PRINCIPLES
OF
APPRAISAL

PRINCIPLES
OF
APPRAISAL

ONTARIO REAL ESTATE ASSOCIATION

The Ontario Real Estate Association wishes to express its gratitude to all of the members and staff who have contributed to the development of this publication. A special note of thanks goes to Mr. Joseph P. Abela and Mr. Kai Stub, primary authors of this text.

International Standard Book Number
0-919-483-18-6

Typesetting by Moravia Publication Services and The House of Lind
Printed and Bound in Canada by T. H. Best Printing Company Limited

Preface

Appraisal of real property can rightfully be considered the very foundation of all real estate activity. Whether a person is investing, developing, lending, renting, exchanging, buying or selling real estate a working knowledge of sound valuation principles is paramount in order to estimate market value.

Aside from being a specialized field of real estate activity, appraising is a most important requirement and a significant adjunct to the brokerage business. To anyone dealing with real estate on a day-to-day basis, particularly real estate brokers and their sales people, a basic knowledge of appraising is all but indispensable.

It is a fundamental principle that a comprehensive knowledge of one's product is basic to effective marketing. Not only must the broker and salespeople be completely familiar with the physical aspects of the properties they list, they must also be reasonably qualified to estimate the value of the property in the market place. Probably the question most often asked of real estate practitioners by their clients is "how much is my property worth?"

Though real estate practitioners are not usually required to submit a written report substantiating their opinion of value each time they list a property, nevertheless, they do have the duty to advise and counsel their clients intelligently as to the probable selling price of the property. They cannot do this unless they have a reasonably good understanding of the appraisal process and the ability to apply the various appraisal techniques.

Contents

CHAPTER 6: STEP SIX.
APPLICATION OF THE DIRECT SALES
COMPARISON APPROACH. 119

Glossary
of
Appraisal Terminology

Abstraction Method The allocation of the appraised total value of the property between land and building. This may be accomplished either on a ratio basis or by subtracting a figure representing building value from the appraised total value of the improved property. Although a distribution or allocation of a price or value between land/improvement by statistical ratios can be useful at times, the procedure has limitations.

Accruals for Depreciation Provisions for (usually credits to reserves on accounting statements) anticipated depreciation.

Accrued Depreciation The difference between reproduction cost new or replacement cost new of the improvements and the present worth of those improvements, both measured as of the date of appraisal. In measuring accrued depreciation, the appraiser is interested in identifying and measuring the loss in utility experienced by the subject structure in its present condition, as compared to the utility it would have as a new improvement representing the highest and best use of the site. Accrued depreciation is sometimes referred to as diminished utility.

Acre A measure of land equalling 160 square rods, or 4,840 square yards, 43,560 square feet, or .4 hectares.

Actual Age	The number of years elapsed since an original structure was built. Sometimes referred to as historical or chronological age.
Adverse Possession	When an individual, not the owner, takes actual possession of the property, hostile to, and without the consent of the owner.
Age-Life Method	A method of estimating accrued depreciation as a percentage applied to current reproduction cost new of the improvements. The percentage reflects the ratio of estimated effective age to typically anticipated economic life but may also be computed as the ratio of effective age to the sum of the effective age plus estimated remaining economic life. The Age-Life Method may also be applied to current replacement cost new of improvements in which case the percentage calculated may differ from that percentage used for application to current reproduction cost new of improvements.
Age-Life Method, Modified	A method of estimating accrued depreciation which recognizes the possibility of curing certain items of accrued depreciation. The cost to cure all curable items, both physical and functional, is estimated, and this sum is deducted from reproduction cost new of the improvements. A percentage lump-sum deduction covering all incurable items is then derived by applying to the remaining reproduction cost new of the improvements a percentage computed by the Age-Life Method.
Agent	One who is authorized by a principal to represent him in business transactions with a third party. In the real estate profession it refers to a broker.
Agreement of Purchase and Sale	A contract by which one party agrees to sell and another agrees to purchase.

Agreement to Lease   A contract by which one party agrees to rent real estate to another party for a rental fee or other compensation.

Amenities   The pleasant satisfactions that are received through using rights in real property but that are not received in the form of money. The tangible and intangible benefits generated by a property.

Amortization   The gradual retirement of a debt by means of partial payments of the principal at regular intervals.

Anticipation, Principle of   Affirms that value is created by the anticipation of future benefits. (Value may be defined as the present worth of all rights to future benefits.)

Appraisal   An estimate or opinion of value. The act or process of estimating value. The resulting opinion of value derived from the appraisal may be informal, transmitted orally; or it may be formal, presented in written form. Usually it is a written statement setting forth an opinion of the value of an adequately described property as of a specified date, supported by the presentation and analysis of relevant data. Synonym: valuation.

Appraisal Date   The date as of which the value estimate is applicable and valid. The date of appraisal identifies the market conditions that existed when the appraisal was made.

Appraisal Process   A systematic analysis of the factors that bear upon the value of real estate. An orderly program by which the problem is defined, the work necessary to solve the problem is planned, and the data involved are acquired, classified, analyzed, and interpreted into an estimate of value.

Appraisal Report Although abbreviated forms of appraisal reports (including verbal) may be acceptable depending upon the requirements of the client, the type of property, and the nature of the appraisal assignment, the narrative appraisal report is a formal written document which contains (a) the estimate of value, (b) the effective date of the appraisal, (c) the certification and signature of the appraiser, (d) the purpose of the appraisal, (e) the qualifying conditions, (f) an adequate description of the neighbourhood and identification of the property and its ownership, (g) the factual data, (h) an analysis and interpretation of the data, (i) the processing of the data by one or more of the three approaches and (j) other descriptive supporting material (maps, plans, charts, photographs).

Appraiser One who estimates value; specifically, one who possesses the necessary qualifications, ability, and experience to execute or direct the appraisal of real or personal property. See also Professional Appraiser.

Appreciation Increase in value due to increase in cost to reproduce, value over the cost, or value at some specified earlier point in time, brought about by greater demand, improved economic conditions, increasing price levels, reversal of depreciating environmental trends, improved transportation facilities, direction of community or area growth, or other factors.

Appurtenance Something which is outside the real property itself, but belongs to the land and is joined thereto. It adds to greater enjoyment of the land. A right-of-way is an appurtenance.

Arm's Length	A transaction freely arrived at in the open market, unaffected by abnormal pressure or by the absence of normal competitive negotiation as might be true in the case of a transaction between related parties.
Assemblage	The combining of two or more contiguous parcels into one ownership or use. See also Plottage.
Assessed Value	A valuation placed upon property by the province, as a basis for municipal taxation.
Assessor	An official who has the responsibility of determining assessed value for tax purposes.
Assumption of Mortgage	The taking of title to property by a grantee, wherein he assumes liability for an existing mortgage against a property and becomes personally liable for the payment of such mortgage debt.
Balance, Principle of	Holds that value is created and maintained in proportion to the equilibrium attained in the amount and location of essential uses of real estate. The degree of value of a property is governed by the balance or apportionment of the four factors in production.
Breach of Contract	Failure to fulfill an obligation under a contract. Breach confers a right of action on the offended party.
Building Residual Technique	The process of estimating the contribution of improvements to the present worth or value of the entire property, over and above the value of the site, in which: (1) Return attributable to the land, valued independently of the building, is deducted from Net Operating Income; and (2) The residual income, representing return to the building (including recapture) is capitalized to indicate building value.

Building Permit		A document issued by the municipal authority certifying the blueprints for construction and allowing work to commence.
Bundle of Rights		A concept in which rights of possession, use, enjoyment, and disposition comprise the rights of ownership.
Capitalization		The process of converting into present value (or obtaining the present worth of) a series of anticipated future periodic installments of net income. In real estate appraising, it usually takes the form of discounting.
Capitalization Rate		The sum of a Discount Rate and a Capital Recapture Rate. It is applied to any income stream with a finite term over which the invested principal is to be returned to the investor or lender.

Capitalization

The process of converting into present value (or obtaining the present worth of) a series of anticipated future periodic installments of net income. In real estate appraising, it usually takes the form of discounting.

Capitalization Rate

The sum of a Discount Rate and a Capital Recapture Rate. It is applied to any income stream with a finite term over which the invested principal is to be returned to the investor or lender.

The term "Capitalization Rate" (Cap Rate) has been traditionally used colloquially in reference to overall rate. Proper terminology would distinguish between these two terms and avoid the colloquial usage of the term "Cap Rate."

Change, Principle of

Holds that economic and social forces are constantly at work and because changes brought about by these forces affect real property, the appraiser views real property and its environment as in transition, observing evidence of trends which may affect the property in the future. The law of change is fundamentally the law of cause and effect.

Contract

A contract is a legally binding agreement between two or more capable persons for consideration or value, to do or not to do some lawful and genuinely intended act.

Contract Rent

Payment for the use of property as designated in a lease. Used to establish the fact that the actual rent designated, or contract rent, may differ from market rent.

Contribution, Principle of

A valuation principle which states that the value of an agent of production or of a component part of a property depends upon how much it contributes to the value of the whole; or how much its absence detracts from the value of the whole. The Principle of Contribution is sometimes known as the Principle of Marginal Productivity. See also Increasing and Diminishing Returns.

Cost

The price paid or obligated for anything. The amount of money or its equivalent worth which is exchanged for use of ownership of property. See also, Replacement Cost and Reproduction Cost.

Cost Approach

That approach in appraisal analysis which is based on the proposition that the informed purchaser would pay no more than the cost of producing a substitute property with the same utility as the subject property. It is particularly applicable when the property being appraised involves relatively new improvements which represent the highest and best use of the land or when relatively unique or specialized improvements are located on the site and for which there exist no comparable properties on the market.

Cost Estimating

In construction, the cost to build based on a quantity survey of the cost of all materials and labour to be employed and other essential costs incurred in the process. In appraising, estimating the reproduction or replacement cost of an improvement by one of several methods. See also Quantity-Survey Method and Unit-in-Place Method.

Conveyance	The transfer of an interest in property from one person to another.
Covenant	An agreement contained in a deed and creating an obligation. It may be positive, stipulating the performance of some act.
Curable Depreciation	Those items of physical deterioration and functional obsolescence which are economically feasible to cure and hence are customarily repaired or replaced by a prudent property owner. The estimate of this depreciation is usually computed as a dollar amount of the cost-to-cure.
Deed	An instrument in writing, duly executed and delivered, that conveys title or an interest in real property.
Deed Restriction	An imposed restriction in a deed for the purpose of limiting the use of the land.
Depreciation	A loss in value due to any cause.
Deterioration	Impairment of condition; one of the causes of depreciation, reflecting the loss in value brought about by wear and tear, disintegration, use in service, and the action of the elements. Also, synonymous with physical depreciation which may be further classified as curable or incurable depreciation. See also Depreciation, Curable Depreciation, Incurable Depreciation.
Direct Sales Comparison Approach	That approach in appraisal analysis which is based on the proposition that an informed purchaser would pay no more for a property than the cost to him of acquiring an existing property with the same utility. This approach is applicable when an active market provides sufficient quantities of reliable data which can be verified from authoritative sources. The direct sales com-

parison approach is relatively unreliable in an inactive market or in estimating the value of properties for which no real comparable sales data are available. It is also questionable when sales data cannot be verified with principals to the transaction. Also referred to as the Market Comparison or Market Data Approach.

Easement
A right enjoyed by one landowner over the land of another.

Economic Life
The period over which improvements to real estate contribute to the value of the property. This establishes the capital recovery period for improvements in the traditional residual techniques of income capitalization. It is also used in the estimation of accrued depreciation (diminished utility) in the Cost Approach to value estimation. See also Remaining Economic Life.

Effective Age
As applied to a structure, the age of a similar structure of equivalent utility, condition, and remaining life expectancy as distinct from chronological age; the years of age indicated by the condition and utility of the structure. If a building has had better than average maintenance, its effective age may be less than the actual age; if there has been inadequate maintenance, it may be greater. A 40-year old building may have an effective age of 20 years due to rehabilitation or modernization.

Effective Gross Income
The estimated Potential Gross Income less Allowance for Vacancy and Income Loss plus Other Income. The anticipated income from all operations of the real estate after allowance for vacancy and income loss.

Encroachment
The unauthorized extension of the boundaries of land.

Encumbrance	Outstanding claim or lien recorded against property or any legal right to the use of the property by another person who is not the owner.
Engineering Breakdown Method	A method of estimating accrued depreciation under which separate estimates are made for the individual components and then totalled.
Escheat	The reversion of property to the state in the event the owner thereof dies leaving no will and having no legally qualified heir to whom the property may pass by lawful descent.
Estate	An interest in land.
Ethics	Rules of behaviour made and accepted by business to provide fair and moral practice.
Expense Ratio	The ratio of expenses to gross income; the fraction of gross income consumed by expenses; normally, in appraisal practice, the ratio of stabilized expenses to projected effective gross income.
Expropriation	Taking of private property by the state for public use, with fair compensation to the owner, through the exercise of the right of eminent domain.
Factors or Agents in Production	The factors in the production of wealth, income or services which can be sold for money. The factors are: (1) labour, (2) management (coordination), (3) capital, (4) land (or natural resources). Of the gross income from any enterprise, labour has the first claim. The cost of labour are wages, salaries, and cost of benefits, such as health insurance, unemployment insurance, etc. After labour are the costs of coordination, (entrepreneurial incentive together with those services necessary to coordinate the offices of the other three factors and weld them into a productive unit) and the costs of capital, by

which is meant payment for the use of capital, interest on and amortization of the investment in buildings, equipment, furnishings, etc., but not land. Then last, and least in order of preference, is the claim of land to the residual portion of the gross income.

Fee Simple

The highest estate or absolute right in real property.

Fixed Expenses (Charges)

Those expenses that do not vary with occupancy (e.g. ad valorem taxes and fire insurance) and that have to be paid whether the property is occupied or vacant. Fixed expenses are not necessarily or absolutely fixed in amount, and tend to vary from year to year.

Functional Curable Obsolescence

Functional obsolescence which may be corrected or cured when the cost of replacing the outmoded or unacceptable component is at least offset by the anticipated increase in utility, and, hence, ultimately in value, resulting from the replacement.

Functional Incurable Obsolescence

Functional obsolescence that results from structural deficiencies or superadequacies that the prudent purchaser or owner would not be justified in replacing, adding or removing, because the cost of effecting a cure would be greater than the anticipated increase in utility resulting from the replacement, addition, or removal.

Functional Obsolescence

Impairment of functional capacity or efficiency. Functional obsolescence reflects the loss in value brought about by such factors as overcapacity, inadequacy, and changes in the art, that affect the property item itself or its relation with other items comprising a larger property. The inability of a structure to perform adequately the function for which it is currently employed.

Functional Utility
The sum of the attractiveness and usefulness of the property. It is the ability of the property to perform the function for which it is intended, in terms of current market tastes and standards. Elements of functional utility in a residence include architecture, design and layout, traffic pattern, sizes and types of rooms, and performance standards.

Function of the Appraisal
The reason for which the appraisal is made or is intended to be used. Relates to the character of the decision to be based on the appraisal, e.g., price at which to buy or sell, amount of mortgage to be made. Not the same as Purpose.

Grant
A technical term used in deeds of conveyance to indicate a transfer of an interest or estate in land.

Grantee
The party to whom an interest in real property is conveyed.

Grantor
The party who conveys an interest in real property by deed.

Gross Income (Rent) Multiplier
The relationship (ratio) between sales price (value) and either Potential Gross Income or Effective Gross Income—these relationships are not to be intermingled, i.e., there must be consistency in the method of computing multipliers used for analysis. It is used to estimate value as a multiple of annual gross income (potential or effective).

Hoskold Factor
A multiplier obtained by calculation or from special tables which is used to capitalize income produced by a wasting asset. The Hoskold factor provides for recapture by actual or hypothetical contributions to a sinking fund which grows with compound interest at a "safe

rate.'' In addition, the Hoskold factor provides for ''return on'' the investment at a higher ''speculative rate.''

Income Approach
That procedure in appraisal analysis which converts anticipated benefits (dollar income or amenities) to be derived from the ownership of property into a value estimate. The income approach is widely applied in appraising income-producing properties. Anticipated future income and/or reversions are discounted to a present worth figure through the capitalization process.

Increasing and Decreasing (Diminishing Returns)
A valuation principle which states that when successive increments of one or more factors of production are added to fixed amounts of the other factors there is a resulting enhancement of income (in dollars, benefits, or amenities), initially at an increasing rate to a point of maximum return and then decreasing until eventually the increment to value becomes increasingly less than the value of the added factor (or factors). The Principle of Increasing and Decreasing Returns is sometimes known as the Principle of Diminishing Returns or the Principle of Variable Proportions.

Incurable Depreciation
Elements of physical deterioration or functional obsolescence which either cannot be corrected, or, if possible to correct, cannot be corrected except at a cost in excess of their contribution to the value of the property.

Joint Tenancy
Ownership of land by two or more persons whereby, on the death of one, the survivor or survivors take the whole estate.

Joist
One of a series of horizontal wood members, usually 2-inch nominal thickness, used to support a floor, ceiling or roof.

Judgment	The decision of the court.
Landlord	The person from whom another holds tenancy.
Land Residual Technique	A valuation technique which presumes that income can be split between land and improvements and that the residual to land can then be capitalized into value. Typically, the building is valued independently of the land, and the annual return on the building value (return on investment and provision for capital recapture) is deducted from the anticipated Net Operating Income to the property (land and building). The residual amount is said to be attributable to the land and is capitalized at the appropriate Risk (Discount) Rate to indicate the land value. For new structures, the value assigned to the building is cost, which assumes no accrued depreciation and construction at a proper current cost. If reasonably new and subject to minimal depreciation which can be satisfactorily estimated, the assigned value is the depreciated value as of the date of appraisal.

In the case of an old structure it is preferable to assume the construction cost and rental income for a hypothetical new and proper structure as the basis for estimating the net income attributable to the land. |
Lease	Contract between landlord (lessor) and tenant (lessee) for the occupation or use of the landlord's property by the tenant for a specified time and for a specified consideration (rental).
Legal Description	A written description by which property can be located, definitely.
Lessee	Tenant under a lease.
Lessor	The person who grants use of property under lease to a tenant.

Lien	A right, given to a creditor, creating an interest in the real property until the debt is discharged.
Locational (Extrinsic) Obsolescence	That loss in value experienced by a structure as a result of negative environmental forces outside the boundaries of the property. Is also known as environmental obsolescence or economic obsolescence.
Long-lived Items	Those basic structural components which in the normal course of events have economic lives as long as the economic life of the entire structure.
Market Price	The amount actually paid, or to be paid, for a property in a particular transaction. Differs from market value in that it is an accomplished or historic fact, whereas market value is and remains an estimate until proved. Market price involves no assumption of prudent conduct by the parties, or absence of undue stimulus or of any other condition basic to the market value concept.
Market Rent	The rental income that a property would most probably command on the open market as indicated by current rentals being paid for comparable space (as of the effective date of appraisal). This is preferred terminology to the term "Economic Rent" which has traditionally been used in appraisal analysis, even though both are currently considered synonymous.
Market Value	(Formal Definition) The highest price in terms of money, which the property will bring to a willing seller if exposed for sale on the open market allowing a reasonable time to find a willing purchaser, buying with the knowledge of all the uses to which it is adapted and for which it is legally capable of being used, and with neither party acting under necessity, compulsion or peculiar and special circumstances.

Metes and Bounds	A system of land description whereby all boundary lines are set forth by use of terminal points and angles—mete referring to a limit or limiting mark, and bounds referring to boundary lines.
Modernization	Taking corrective measures to bring a property into conformity with changes in style, whether exterior or interior or additions necessary to meet standards of current demand. It normally involves replacing parts of the structure or mechanical equipment with modern replacements of the same kind and hence seldom includes capital improvements.
More or Less	Term often found in a property description intended to cover slight, unimportant or unsubstantial inaccuracies of which both parties are willing to assume the risk.
Mortgage	A conveyance of property to a creditor as security for payment of a debt with a right of redemption upon payment of the debt.
Mortgagee	The one to whom property is conveyed as security for the payment of a debt; the lender or creditor.
Mortgage-Equity	Capitalization and investment analysis procedures which recognize the influence of mortgage terms and equity requirements in the valuation of income properties.
Mortgagor	The one who makes the mortgage; the borrower or debtor.
Neighbourhood	A portion of a larger community, or an entire community, in which there is a homogenous grouping of inhabitants, buildings, or business enterprises. Inhabitants of a neighbourhood usually have a more than casual community of interest and a similarity of economic level or

cultural background. Neighbourhood boundaries may consist of well-defined natural or man-made barriers or they may be more or less well-defined by a distinct change in land use or in the character of the inhabitants.

Net Operating Income (NOI)

Annual net income remaining after deducting all fixed and operating expenses but before deducting financial charges such as recapture or debt service; same as annual dividend. In mortgage-equity formulas, designated by the symbol d. Sometimes referred to as Net Income Before Recapture (NIBR) or Net Income Before Depreciation (NIBD).

Observed Condition Method

A method of estimating accrued depreciation which considers and estimates separately the deductions for physical deterioration, functional obsolescence and locational obsolescence. The several estimates are then added to provide a lump-sum deduction from reproduction cost new.

Obsolescence

One of the causes of depreciation. It is the impairment of desirability and usefulness brought about by new inventions, current changes in design, and improved processes for production, or from external influencing factors, which make a property less desirable and valuable for a continued use. Obsolescence may be either economic or functional. See also Depreciation, Locational Obsolescence, Functional Obsolescence.

Operating Expenses

Generally denotes all expenses necessary to maintain the production of income from operation of a property; the difference between Effective Gross Income and Net Operating Income (NOI). Also used to denote a category of expense exclusive of fixed expense, debt service, depreciation allowance and reserves for replacements.

Overall Rate	The direct ratio between Annual Net Operating Income (NOI) and Value or Sales Price. Denoted by symbol R or the formula d/v in the Elwood formulation.
Personal Property	All property, except land and the improvements thereon.
Physical Curable Deterioration	Physical deterioration which the prudent buyer would anticipate correcting upon purchase of the property. The cost of effecting the correction or cure would be no more than the anticipated addition to utility, and hence ultimately to value, associated with the cure. Curable physical deterioration is frequently termed "deferred maintenance" or rehabilitation, because these terms reflect the type of activity typically associated with correcting the condition.
Physical Deterioration	A reduction in utility resulting from an impairment of physical condition. For purposes of appraisal analysis, it is most common and convenient to divide physical deterioration into curable and incurable components.
Physical Incurable Deterioration	Physical deterioration which in terms of market conditions as of the date of the appraisal it is not feasible or economically justified to correct. The cost of correcting the condition or effecting a cure is estimated to be greater than the anticipated increase in utility, and hence ultimately in value, of the property that will result from correcting or curing the condition. For purposes of appraisal analysis, incurable physical deterioration may be divided into short-lived and long-lived elements.
Plottage	The process of assembling two or more sites under a single ownership such that there is an increment derived from greater utility. See also Plottage Value.

Potential Gross Income	The income that a property will produce with 100% occupancy. The potential gross income is generally derived by multiplying the rental value per unit times the number of units in the building.
Property Residual Technique	A capitalization technique in which the Net Operating Income is considered attributable to the property as a whole rather than divided into land and building components. In annuity capitalization, this technique involves computation of the present worth of an income stream to which is added the present worth of a reversion at its assumed termination.
Purpose of the Appraisal	The type of value being sought. Not the same as Function.
Quantity-Survey Method	A method of construction cost or reproduction cost estimating. In its strictest application it is a repetition of the contractor's original procedure of estimating the quantity and grade of each type of material used in the structure, estimating labour hours required, and applying unit costs to the material and labour quantities, with additional allowance for such items of indirect costs as overhead costs, labour, insurance, and contractor's profit. The quantity survey, although still an estimate, is the most accurate and provable method. However, it is time-consuming to prepare and its general use is confined to contractors and in the valuation of public utility and special-purpose properties.
Quit Claim Deed	A general release of all claims or rights to a parcel of land.
Real Estate	"Real Estate" includes real property, lease-hold and business whether with or without premises, fixtures, stock-in-trade, goods or chattels in connection with the operation of the business. (Real Estate and Business Brokers Act)

Real Property	The combination of the tangible and intangible attributes of land and improvements. Value-wise, it is the sum of the value of the real estate, considered as land and structure and, for example, the tangible value arising by reason of a favourable lease. The real estate, plus the rights that go with it.
Reconciliation	The process by which the appraiser evaluates, chooses and selects from among two or more alternative conclusions or indications to reach a single answer (final value estimate). Preferable terminology to the traditional term ''correlation.''
Reconstructed Operating Statement	A statement usually prepared by an appraiser from figures obtained from numerous sources including an auditor's statement which, in the appraiser's opinion, reflects the probable future Net Operating Income and is in keeping with the quantity and quality of services anticipated in the stabilized income estimated by the appraiser.
Rehabilitation	The restoration of a property to satisfactory condition without changing the plan, form, or style of a structure. In urban renewal, the restoration to good condition of deteriorated structures, neighbourhoods, and public facilities. Neighbourhood rehabilitation encompasses structural rehabilitation, and in addition may extend to street improvements and a provision of such amenities as parks and playgrounds.
Remaining Economic Life	The number of years remaining in the economic life of the structure or structural component, as of the date of the appraisal. In part a function of the attitudes and reactions of typical buyers in the market, and in part, a function of the market reactions to competitive properties on the market.

Remodelling	Changing the plan, form, or style of a structure to correct functional or economic deficiencies.
Replacement Cost	The cost of construction at current prices of a building having utility equivalent to the building being appraised but built with modern materials and according to current standards, design and layout. The use of the replacement cost concept presumably eliminates all functional obsolescence, and the only depreciation to be measured is physical deterioration and economic obsolescence.
Reproduction Cost	The cost of construction at current prices of an exact duplicate or replica using the same materials, construction standards, design, layout, and quality of workmanship, embodying all the deficiencies, superadequacies and obsolescence of the subject building.
Restrictive Covenant	A limitation placed upon the use of property, contained in the deed.
Right	The interest one has in a piece of property.
Right of Survivorship	The distinguishing feature of joint tenancies which provides that, where land is held in undivided portions by co-owners, upon the death of any joint owner, his interest in the land will pass to the surviving co-owner, rather than to his estate.
Servient Tenement	Land over which an easement exists in favour of the dominant tenement.
Set Back	The distance from the curb or other established line within which no buildings may be erected.

Short-Lived Items	Those components or elements of a structure or items of equipment whose remaining economic lives are shorter or are expected to be shorter than the remaining economic life of the entire structure.
Sinking Fund	A fund in which periodic deposits of equal amounts of money are made for the purpose of ultimately paying a debt, or replacing assets. Usually it is a fund in which is placed equal annual or monthly deposits which, with compound interest thereon, will accumulate to a predetermined amount at the end of a stated period of time.
Site	A parcel of land which is improved to the extent that it is ready for use for the purpose for which it is intended.
Site Analysis	The identification and analysis of the characteristics that create, enhance or detract from the utility and marketability of a site.
Substitution, Principle of	A valuation principle that states that a prudent purchaser would pay no more for real property than the cost of acquiring an equally desirable substitute on the open market. The Principle of Substitution presumes that the purchaser will consider the alternatives available to him, that he will act rationally or prudently on the basis of his information about those alternatives, and that time is not a significant factor. Substitution may assume the form of the purchase of an existing property, with the same utility, or of acquiring an investment which will produce an income stream of the same size with the same risk as that involved in the property in question.

Superadequacy

A greater capacity or quality in the structure or one of its components than the prudent purchaser or owner would include or would pay for in the particular type of structure under current market conditions.

Supply and Demand, Principle of

A valuation principle which states that market value is determined by the interaction of the forces of supply and demand in the appropriate market as of the date of the appraisal.

Surplus Productivity

The net income that remains after the proper costs of labour, organization, and capital have been paid, which surplus is imputable to the land and tends to fix the value thereof.

Tenancy-in-Common

Ownership of land by two or more persons; unlike joint tenancy in that interest of deceased does not pass to the survivor, but is treated as an asset of the deceased's estate.

Tenant

One who occupies land or tenement under a landlord.

Tenure

A system of land holdings for a temporary time period.

Unit-in-Place Method

A method of estimating construction costs which involves estimating the unit cost of component sections of the structure installed or "in place." The unit includes both materials and labour.

Units of Comparison

The reduction of properties to appropriate units in terms of which comparisons of otherwise not directly comparable properties can be made. These units of comparison can then be applied to individual properties to formulate estimates of value, income, cost, etc. Ideally, they should represent units in terms of which properties are in fact sold, rented, built, or valued.

Useful Life	The period of time over which the structure may reasonably be expected to perform the function for which it was designed or intended.
Value	The quantity of one thing which can be obtained in exchange for another: the ratio of exchange of one commodity for another, e.g., one bushel of wheat in terms of a given number of bushels of corn; thus, the value of one thing may be expressed in terms of another. Money is the common denominator by which real property value is usually measured.
	It is the power of acquiring commodities in exchange, generally with a comparison of utilities—the utility of the commodity acquired in the exchange (property).
	Value also depends upon the relation of an object to unsatisfied needs; i.e., scarcity of supply and demand.
	Value is the present worth of future benefits arising out of ownership to typical users or investors.
Value in Exchange	The amount of goods and services or purchasing power which an informed purchaser would offer in exchange for an economic good under given market conditions. Value in exchange is relative, as there must be a comparison with other economic good or goods, and alternatives available from which the potential purchaser may make his choice.
Value in Use	The value of an economic good to its owner-user which is based on the productivity (privacies in income, utility or amenity form) of the economic good to a specific individual; subjective value. May not necessarily represent market value.

Introduction

Appraisal and
Real Estate Fundamentals

Nature of Appraisals and Appraising

Appraisal of real estate is a fascinating, many-sided enterprise bringing the appraiser into contact with many different business experiences and people from all walks of life. Estimations of market value are the most frequent type of appraisal assignments, however, because of their specialized training and experience, appraisers are often called upon to provide a wide variety of additional appraisal services: highest and best use and feasibility studies for land development, investment analysis, estimating leases through property expropriation, forecasting the cash flow of proposed commercial developments, real estate consulting—these and other appraisal functions fall within the scope of the appraiser's work.

Appraising, therefore, is problem solving. It involves, firstly, the ability to define and isolate the problem; and secondly, the gathering, analysis and application of relevant market data to reach a valid conclusion.

An appraisal is an estimate of value based on what is taking place in the market. It can be given orally but it is usally a written statement of market value, or other value as defined by the appraiser, of an adequately described property as of a specific date.

It becomes apparent that, in a general sense, everyone is a real estate appraiser at some point in time. Anyone who has ever bought or sold a house, or who owns or has owned real estate, has formed his own opinion about the value of that particular piece of real estate in order to reach a decision. This general category could be classified as the first level of appraisal knowledge.

The second level involves real estate brokers and sales people, developers, mortgage lenders and others whose business requires them to deal on a day-to-day basis with real estate and form opinions about value. They, by their experience and training, are in a better position to know the real estate market and form more competent and objective opinions about values.

At the third level is the specialist or the professional appraiser who spends a lifetime acquiring the knowledge and skills necessary to write objective reports dealing with estimates of value for clients in levels one and two who do not feel competent or qualified to form, express and support their own opinions.

An appraiser, whether from level one, two or three, considers historical data in order to forecast future probabilities (i.e. estimate value). It is important, at this point, to emphasize that the appraiser does *not* "set" or "establish" the value. He only studies the market and the historical data and attempts to predict the *probable* selling price of a particular piece of property.

A real estate appraiser is a real estate specialist. He is an objective observer whose training, knowledge, skill and experience are brought to play on real estate problems requiring an unbiased estimate of value.

APPRAISAL COMPETENCE

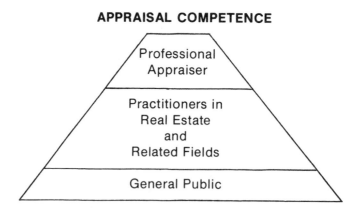

cost approach best for new bldgs.

The Nature of Value

Value is a key word that is utilized in practically every segment of the real estate business. Its significance and importance would imply that its meaning be precisely and clearly understood. Unfortunately this is often not the case. Value is a word of many meanings and there are as many definitions as there are types of value in everyday usage. For example, the tax assessor usually thinks of value in terms of *assessed value*, the insurance agent in terms of *insurable value*, and the accountant in terms of *book value*. The banker or mortgagee is likely to equate value with *loan value*. So there is a natural tendency to attach to the word "value" a variety of descriptive adjectives suggesting a specific kind of value. For instance, one might refer to market value, assessed value, book value, appraisal value, monetary value, sentimental value, salvage value, liquidation value, and intrinsic value, to name just a few. In appraisal work, it is essential that there be a clear understanding of the nature of the value being sought.

The precise meaning of the word value has been a life-long study of many economic theorists. Among those who have contributed to the evolution of the value concept, some have argued that value is an objective concept, while others maintained that it is subjective.

In real estate appraising the **objective value** concept maintains that *(COMMERCIAL)* value is tied up in the cost of production or cost of creating the property. Affirming that value is inherent in the object valued and dependent upon the cost of its making, forms the basis for the cost approach to value.

The **subjective value** concept affirms that value is created and exists only in the mind of the potential buyers, sellers, owners and users of real estate. It is the price that people will pay for a property, irrespective of its cost. The appraiser uses this concept to estimate market value using two of the three recognized approaches to value: namely the Direct Sales Comparison Approach and the Income Approach, both of *(RESIDENTIAL)* which will be discussed fully in later chapters in this text. It is this "subjective" value concept which dominates in real estate valuation. It can matter little what it may have cost to develop a property; its value is measured through the present worth of all the future benefits that likely will accrue through its ownership. Future benefits do not necessarily indicate money as with an income stream; they can also indicate such subjective factors as pleasurable living as in the case of a house, or amenities as in the case of a park or a forest reserve. The value of the property is to be found in the satisfaction it offers, and its ratio of exchange in the market can be measured in terms of money.

Categories of Value

As has already been stated, value can have different meanings. One of the many distinctions in defining value is that between "value in exchange" and "value in use." The distinction here is that a property may have one value in exchange and quite a different value in use.

Value in Exchange maintains that value is the probable price at which an economic commodity exchanges on a free, competitive and open market. Therefore, value in exchange is synonymous with market value in real estate appraisal.

Value in Use is the value of a property designed to fit the particular requirements or needs of a specific owner (sometimes known as Value to the Owner). This type of value is usually difficult to measure objectively because in most cases there is no pattern of market behaviour available. When there is value in use, its measure is market value plus a special value to the owner.

One of the most commonly used examples of value in use is that of a house outfitted for an owner confined to a wheelchair. The house has a ramp up the stairs, kitchen cupboards constructed to a convenient height and other such alterations. To this handicapped owner, the house takes on an element of value over and above that which it could likely command in the market; it has convenience and utility and it gives the owner satisfaction. Nevertheless, viewed from a market standpoint those "extras" could well cause a loss in value of the property since they are not desired by most purchasers.

Market Value — *THE HIGHEST PROBABLE SELLING PRICE. that a property will bring if exposed in an open market for a reasonable length of time sold by a willing seller to a willing & knowledgeable purchaser neither party acting under duress.*

By far, the most sought after value in real estate appraisal is the market value of the property. It is the price (value in exchange) that would tend to prevail or occur as a result of the interaction of the forces of supply and demand, under the market conditions existing as of the date of appraisal.

Numerous definitions of market value have been devised over the years by professional appraisal organizations, government bodies, courts and authors of appraisal theory. Among the most widely accepted definitions are the following:

> **Federal Expropriation Act:** *The amount that would have been paid for the interest if, at the time of its taking, it had been sold in the open market by a willing seller to a willing buyer.*
>
> **Ontario Expropriation Act:** *The amount that the land might be*

expected to realize if sold in the open market by a willing seller to a willing buyer.

Real Estate Appraisal Terminology—sponsored jointly by the American Institute of Real Estate Appraisers and the Society of Real Estate Appraisers: *The highest price in terms of money which a property will bring in a competitive and open market under all conditions requisite to a fair sale, the buyer and seller, each acting prudently, knowledgeably and assuming the price is not affected by undue stimulus.*

The Appraisal Institute of Canada: *The probable price a property would sell for on the date of appraisal, allowing a reasonable time to find a purchaser.*

Although there are many definitions of market value, they all have certain factors in common and tend to establish an attitude for the appraiser to adopt. In effect, the appraiser is attempting to estimate the price for which the property will sell under average sale circumstances. Average sale circumstances include:

An informed buyer and seller. This includes an awareness of the alternatives that are available to each. The presumption is that they have access to reasonable market information, rather than absolute knowledge.

Rational or prudent behaviour by both buyer and seller. Each is presumed to act in his own self-interest in his buying or selling behaviour.

No undue pressure on either party. A quick or forced sale is not presumed. Neither the buyer nor the seller is acting under compulsion or abnormal pressure.

A reasonable time is allowed to find a buyer. The property must be exposed for sale in the open market for a reasonable length of time.

Quite often the terms market value and market price are mistakenly used interchangeably. Note that there is a distinct difference in the meaning of these two terms.

Market price is the **price** at which any parcel of real estate sells. Market value is the **worth** of that parcel of real estate viewed in the light of the prices at which other comparable parcels of real estate have been sold. Value emerges from *many* sales; price emerges from *every* sale.

Factors or Forces Influencing Real Estate Values

The value of real estate is created, maintained, modified and destroyed by certain factors or forces which may be classified in four categories:

Economic—interest rates, unemployment, wage levels, etc.

Political or Governmental—zoning bylaws, building codes, etc.

Social—recreational and educational facilities, clubs, etc.

Physical—topography, soil, climate, etc.

Basic Principles of Real Property Value

The principles of real estate valuation that influence the way in which the estimation of real property value is approached have evolved from economic doctrine, and are generally accepted as having a direct effect on the modern concept of value. It must be emphasized that these principles rarely, if ever, can be considered in isolation. It is typical to conceive of these principles in an interrelated setting, for they tend to accompany and complement one another. They are presented here independently however, and are in an order which may or may not be in proper sequence for the individual appraisal assignment. These principles are not just academic theories, but keys to an understanding of why, how and when certain things happen. An understanding of them is essential to the proper application of the various techniques and procedures of valuation.

Principle of Supply and Demand

Value or price will react to the change in the supply and demand of any commodity.

If the supply increases but the demand remains constant, price will decrease. If the demand increases but the supply remains constant, price will increase. If both supply and demand increase or decrease proportionately, price will remain relatively stable. The value of real estate tends to be set at the point at which supply and demand equate.

The importance of this principle is obvious when we consider the effect on prices where the supply of new homes is increased without a corresponding increase in demand. Consider the effect on house prices if a large corporation moves its head office and employees from town "A" to town "B." In town "A" prices will fall because of the oversupply while in town "B" prices will rise because of the increase in demand.

Principle of Substitution

When a property is replaceable, its value tends to be set by the cost of acquiring a similar and equally desirable property provided there is no delay in making the acquisition.

This principle is equally applicable in the three most widely used approaches to value.

In the cost approach, a user of real property will pay no more for an existing improved property than the amount that would have to be paid to acquire a suitable site and erect new improvements, providing this can be done within a reasonable and acceptable time period.

In the income approach, an investor will weigh the net income obtainable from any particular property against that obtainable from available substitutes.

In the direct sales comparison approach, a buyer of real property will compare properties offered for sale which provide equivalent utility and will acquire the one which can be purchased at the lowest price, assuming that the acquisition can be made without delay.

A buyer contemplating the purchase of a house for $50,000 would not likely proceed with the transaction if he was aware that, in the same area, there were identical houses being offered for sale at $45,000.

Principle of Highest and Best Use

Fundamental to any appraisal is the selection by the appraiser of the single use that develops the highest value in the subject property. Highest and Best Use is defined as:

That use which, at the time of the appraisal, is most likely to produce the greatest net return, in money or amenities, to the land over a given period of time. Net return may be monetary as with an income producing property or may, in the case of a single family dwelling, take the form of amenities such as pride of ownership, comfort, convenience, etc.

In many instances, the existing use of property is its highest and best use. If this is not so, the appraiser in selecting the highest and best use must ensure that the projected use is one that is permissible, that the property is physically adaptable to it and there is demand for such use.

Principle of Consistent Use

When improved land is in a state of <u>transition</u> to another "highest and best use," it cannot be appraised with one use allocated to the land and another to the building or other improvements.

When an appraiser is estimating the market value of a downtown parcel of land improved with an old house, and estimates that the highest and best use is for an office building development, then he does not accord any value to the house over that of the land. If he did add value for the old house he would, of course, be acting inconsistently; the worth of the house in the market being overshadowed by that of the commercial value of the land. In dealing with compensation for expropriated property, this theory has been referred to as "double recovery."

Principle of Surplus Productivity

Surplus productivity is the net income remaining after all expenses necessary to the operation have been paid and the capital invested in improvements has been satisfied. This remaining net income is imputable to the <u>land</u> and tends to fix its value. As a result, it can be said that the land is valuable according to the surplus productivity imputable to it.

In the operation of an income-producing property, there are three levels of return that are necessary, and a fourth—the land—that can command only the residual income with no fixed or necessary rate of return. These four levels of return are called "The Factors in Production" and must be satisfied in the following order:

> **Labour.** The costs of labour (wages, salaries, Canada Pension, Unemployment Insurance, hospitalization, etc.) must be the first item paid out of the gross income. Both natural law and statute require that labour be paid promptly or it will become unavailable to the property.
>
> **Co-ordination.** After all the costs of labour have been satisfied, the co-ordinating expenses must be paid. These are all the expenses necessary to the proper functioning of the property—public utilities, real estate taxes, insurance premiums, supplies, repairs, etc.
>
> If the costs of public utility services are not paid, they will be discontinued and, as a result, the property becomes unrentable.

For example, if repairs to a building and its equipment are not made, the result would be deterioration and a drop in the gross income. If the insurance premiums are not paid, it may be impossible to keep the building insured and the owner accepts a risk of loss that is not warranted. Thus, the costs of co-ordination must be paid after the claim of labour has been satisfied, but before any income can be assigned to capital or land.

Capital. Capital is the third level of return in the productive rent-producing program. Its claim upon the gross income is subordinate to those of labour or co-ordination but superior to that of the land. If a reasonable return on the capital invested in the improvements on the land is not forthcoming, then the well of funds for such investments will dry up.

Because improvements (buildings, equipment, furnishings, etc.) have a terminable life, there must be both return on and return of capital invested in them.

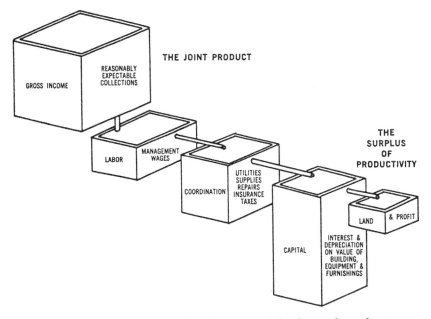

Land, the natural resource. Last in order of the demands made on the income a property produces is the claim of land. There can be no net income to land until the costs of labour, co-ordination and capital have been met, and that is why it is said that land is residual in nature.

It is the surplus income to land that largely determines its value and, with well-developed real estate, the land should yield a reasonable return based on its current realistic value.

A look at an operating statement of an income-producing property will assist in illustrating the principle of surplus productivity.

Example

In this example, it can be assumed that the capital invested in the building is $120,000 and that the return (interest) on the money invested is 10% and that the recapture rate is 2.5%.

Gross annual income received:		$40,000.00
Less: Labour	$ 4,000.00	
Co-ordinating Services	18,000.00	
Requirements on Capital:		
Building—10% interest and		
2.5% recapture (40 years)		
$120,000 × 12.5%	15,000.00	37,000.00
Residual or surplus income		
Attributable to Land		$ 3,000.00

Value of Land $\left(\dfrac{I}{R} = V\right)$ $\dfrac{3,000}{.10}$ = $30,000

✓ **Principle of Contribution** — bond · opts , FP, pools etc.

The value of any component of a property is measured by how much it adds to the net income (or market value if the subject is a single family dwelling) by reason of its presence or detracts from the net income (or market value) by reason of its absence. In other words, the value of any factor in production depends upon its contribution to net income and not upon its cost.

This principle may be illustrated by reference to any program of remodelling or modernization. Any remodelling project of an existing building must so justify itself. For example, the expenditure of $10,000 to convert a basement into an apartment or the addition of a recreation room at a cost of $5,000 is justified only if the result is the production of additional value in excess of the amount spent. Similarly, the installation of modern automatic elevators in place of old ones should increase the net income—by either a reduction in operating expense or an increase in rentals—to some amount in excess of a fair return on, and a recapture of, the cost of installation.

Principle of Increasing and Decreasing Returns — *over improvement*

(DIMINISHING)

Larger and larger amounts of the factors in production will produce greater and greater returns up to a certain point (the law of increasing returns). At this point, the maximum return will have been developed (point of diminishing returns). Any additional expenditure will not produce a return commensurate with these additional investments (the law of decreasing returns).

In an agricultural context, this principle applies in a question of how much fertilizer a farmer should put on his land. Increasing the amount of fertilizer results in a greater yield up to a certain point. Increasing the use of fertilizer beyond this point however does not produce an additional return sufficient to warrant the cost.

In an urban context an appropriate application of this principle would be surplus insulation in a residential property. Up to a certain point the installation of insulation will provide a heat savings in excess of the insulation cost. It is conceivable however that the energy savings will decrease in proportion to the installation of "surplus" insulation.

Principle of Change

Change is a law of life, the law of cause and effect. Nothing in this world remains static. Change is inevitable and is constantly occurring.

Cities, neighbourhoods and individual properties are constantly undergoing the process of change through the evolutionary stages of **Growth**, **Stability** and **Decline**.

The clearest case of change concerning real property is the urban decay and blight which takes such a rapid and costly toll in Canadian cities. The problem of determining highest and best use is compounded by the fact that redevelopment is required long before the actual structures have physically worn out: they are functionally and economically obsolete. This is an extreme illustration of the principle of change, but the appraiser is always observing land use in a state of transition, not in permanence; his best guide to the direction and extent of such transition is the real estate market.

The principle of change illustrates the fact that a value estimate is valid only as of a specific point in time.

Principle of Anticipation *Income Approach*

This principle affirms that value arises by means of the anticipated benefits (money or amenities) to be derived in the future.

When buying a home the buyer anticipates certain benefits that will accrue to him and his family in future years and bases his purchase price on the present worth of those anticipated future benefits.

Principle of Balance *— MONOTONY (WORST) — MIXED STYLES*

Value is created and maintained when there is equilibrium in the amount and location of essential uses of real estate.

Loss in value will result if there are less services and agencies than a neighbourhood needs or more services than a neighbourhood can support. Where there are too many drugstores in a community, for example, either some will be successful at the expense of the others or none will yield an adequate return on the investment they represent.

With an individual property, the agents in production must be in proper balance in order to maintain maximum value. Too much or too little of any one of the agents in production, in proportion to the services rendered by the others, tends to reduce value—for example, having two building custodians where only one is needed will result in less net income, which in turn means less value.

Principle of Conformity

To maintain maximum value, land must be utilized to reasonably conform with the existing standards of the area.

The word *reasonable* is used to denote the degree of conformity. Too much conformity results in monotony, which could be as detrimental to value as not having any conformity at all. In residential areas, variety in the styling of buildings of the same quality presents a more pleasing appearance than rows of identical houses. Zoning regulations should protect a neighbourhood from conversion to or intrusion of inharmonious uses. This principle is particularly useful in detailing a neighbourhood analysis.

RELATED PRINCIPLES *you impeared* *unda impewed*

The **Principle of Regression** and the **Principle of Progression** are extensions of the Principle of Conformity.

The Principle of Regression maintains that between dissimilar properties, the value of the better property will be affected adversely by the presence of the property of lesser value.

For example, in a neighbourhood of $50,000 to $55,000 properties, the value of a $150,000 property tends to regress towards the value of the price level typical of that neighbourhood.

The Principle of Progression is the reverse, affirming that the property of lesser value will be enhanced by proximity to better properties.

A $70,000 property in a neighbourhood of $200,000 homes might sell for more than $70,000 because there are people who cannot afford a $200,000 home, but who will pay a premium to live in a neighbourhood of homes in a higher priced bracket.

Principle of Competition

Excessive profits in any line of business will tend to breed competition which, in turn, tends to destroy profits.

An example of this principle at work would be the situation of the first store in a large shopping centre. It is quite probable that such a store would make fantastic profits. However, it would only be a short time before similar businesses would appear.

Nevertheless, competition is generally considered as a benefit to the real estate trade. It produces increased efficiency in developing and operating properties, economic rents and realistic prices.

Conclusion

There are many factors which must be taken into account when estimating value. The prudent appraiser will carry an indepth knowledge of the various principles and theories which have been formulated over the ages and will use them as reliable tools in the analysis of value and value trends.

Chapter 1

The Appraisal Process

Introduction

The appraisal process is an orderly program or a methodical outline covering the necessary steps in estimating the value of real property. This process the appraiser follows in making the appraisal can be likened to the specific method of solving almost any kind of problem. First, he must consider and analyze the problem and then state clearly and specifically what has to be done. Then he must determine what general and specific data will be required in order to solve the problem. He must then plan the process for gathering, analyzing and classifying the information so it can be considered in the solution to the problem. The next step is to draw conclusions about the solution of the problem in the light of the facts, the problem to be solved and the theory which is applicable. A final consideration is to review the entire process to ensure that all essential facts have been carefully considered and properly treated, and that no errors have been made in calculations. Lastly, a definite statement must be made with respect to the conclusion reached.

To be more specific, the appraisal process contemplates an orderly procedure to be followed in making an appraisal of real property irrespective of type or location. There are seven steps to be followed, as detailed below and illustrated in the diagram that follows.

Steps in the Appraisal Process

1. Definition of the Problem
2. Preliminary Survey and Appraisal Plan

3. Data Collection and Analysis

4. Application of the Cost Approach

5. Application of the Income Approach

6. Application of the Direct Sales Comparison Approach

7. Reconciliation of Value Indications and Final Estimate

Figure 1

The "Appraisal Process" is a seven step process which results in a well defined value estimate. This process may be visualized by comparing it to a funnel. The ingredients of the process are carefully poured into the funnel's mouth. They are individually considered and finally blended into a "market reflected" value estimate.

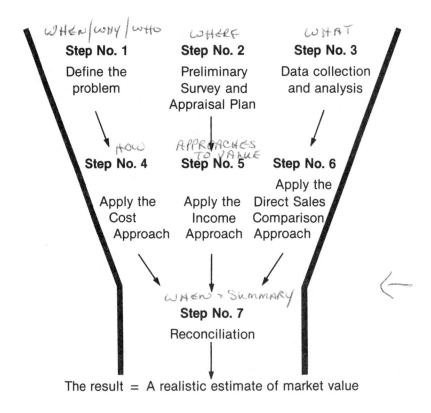

The result = A realistic estimate of market value

Summary

Real estate valuation is not simply a matter of "judgement and experience," but is primarily a matter of logical analysis of subjectively-generated data. It implies that the appraisal process consists of the orderly and systematic solving of the problem. Whether it be a single family home or a large office building, each appraisal is a problem capable of a rational and systematic solution.

Step One
Definition of the Problem

The first step in the appraisal process is to define the problem. Basically, the appraiser must first ascertain the "terms of reference" with respect to the appraisal assignment; in other words, first ascertain *what* must be done, and *why*. This involves consideration of the client's objectives, which in turn establish the appraiser's objectives.

Any ambiguity regarding the appraisal assignment should be eliminated at the start, so that the appraiser knows precisely the nature of the problem beforehand and thereby avoids any possible future misunderstandings with the client. The appraiser does this by identifying or defining the following five basic factors:

The property to be appraised *(pg. 14)*

The property rights involved

The purpose and function of the appraisal

The type of value required

The date of the appraisal.

Identify the Property to be Appraised

It is essential that a complete and accurate identification of the subject property be provided. This identification is achieved by obtaining not only the municipal address, but also the full legal description. For example, the municipal address could be "200 Franklin St., Passville, Ontario." The legal description could be, "Lot 16, Plan 17. City of Passville, Regional Municipality of Grafton."

The legal description is essential to establish accurately the registered land area and location which is to be appraised. Some legal descriptions involve a lot and plan number. This is true in more urbanized areas where a plan of subdivision has been registered.

Where there has been no plan of subdivision registered, the legal description will be by "Metes and Bounds."

When dealing with relatively large tracts of farm lands, the description is usually very simple. These parcels are described as they were originally patented: for example, the entirety of Lot 6, Concession 8, Township of Southwold, County of Elgin; or, the North half of the East half of Lot 6, Concession 8, Township of Southwold, County of Elgin.

For every case there is traditional wording which is used on legal documents:

All and singular that certain parcel or tract of land and premises situate, lying and being in the Township of Southwold, in the County of Elgin and being composed of the whole of Lot 6 in Concession 8 of the said Township.

Such descriptions are quite simple to prepare and the subject property is easily located on the appropriate township map. It would therefore present no problem to explain to a client exactly what land is involved.

An example of a lot and concession description and how it would actually appear on a township map is as follows:

The task of describing a parcel of land that is only part of a lot is not quite so simple. To do this, you must describe the parcel using a **Metes and Bounds** description.

Assume that the parcel you must describe has a 60 foot frontage on concession road 8 and a depth of 150 feet at the south west corner of the lot. This parcel of land would be described as outlined below.

"All and singular that certain parcel or tract of land and premises situate, lying and being in the Township of — — —, more particularly described as follows:

Commencing at the southwest angle of said Lot 6;

thence northerly along the westerly limit of said Lot 6 a distance of 150 feet to a point;

thence easterly, parallel to the southerly limit of said Lot 6 a distance of 60 feet to a point;

thence southerly parallel to the westerly limit of said lot a distance of 150 feet, more or less, to a point in the southerly limit of said lot which point is distance 60 feet measured easterly along said southerly limit from the place of commencement;

thence westerly along the southerly limit a distance of 60 feet, more or less, to the place of commencement."

A sketch of the property would appear as follows:

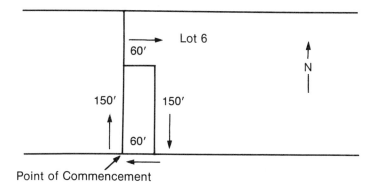

Point of Commencement

You will note that there is always a point of commencement and a reference to a direction contained in a metes and bounds description.

When the subject property has boundaries running parallel to the lot lines then the sketch, such as the one appearing above, is fairly simple to draw. It is quite another matter when the boundaries of the subject property run at different angles than the lot lines. In order to properly describe such a property "Bearings," which really are compass directions, must be used. These directions are always given as east or west of north and east or west of south. An example of this would be:

N 20° W on a survey is written "north 20 degrees west" and simply stated means a line which is 20 degrees west of north.

"S 60° 20′ E" is written "south 60 degrees 20 minutes east" and simply means a line which is 60 degrees twenty minutes east of south.

The entire matter of bearings may be more clearly understood if the reader refers to the diagram which follows:

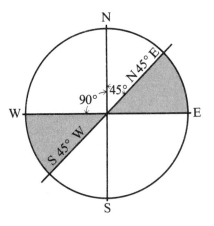

Circles contain 360 degrees, each degree contains 60 minutes and each minute contains 60 seconds.

You will note that each quarter of the circle contains 90 degrees and if you draw a line dividing the quadrant into equal halves then the diagonal line represents a bearing of 45 degrees. (Refer to shaded areas above.) When the diagonal line is proceeding toward the top of the page it is described as 45 degrees east of north (N 45° E). If the line proceeds in the opposite direction it is described as S 45° W, or south, 45 degrees west.

It becomes readily apparent that each line has two different bearings depending on its direction. Very precise property descriptions can be achieved by carefully following a metes and bounds description.

An example of a property described by a metes and bounds would be:

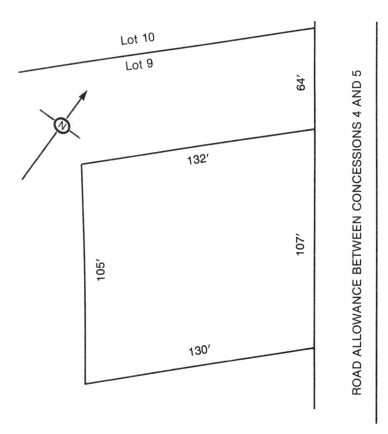

For legal purposes, this property would be described in the following metes and bounds terminology:

"All and singular that certain parcel or tract of land and premises situate, lying and being in the Township of Southwold in the County of Elgin and being composed of part of Lot 9, Concession 4 in said Township, more particularly described as follows:

Premising that the westerly limit of the road allowance between Concessions 4 and 5 has a bearing of north 45 degrees 15 minutes and 32 seconds west and relating all bearings herein thereto;

commencing at a point in the westerly limit of said road allowance distant 64 feet measured on a bearing of south 45 degrees 15 minutes and 32 seconds east along the westerly limit of said road allowance from the northeast angle of said Lot 9;

thence south 35 degrees 15 minutes 23 seconds west a distance of 132 feet to a point;

thence south 48 degrees 13 minutes 48 seconds east a distance of 105 feet to a point;

thence north 40 degrees 21 minutes 55 seconds east a distance of 130 feet more or less to a point in the westerly limit of road allowance;

thence north 45 degrees 15 minutes 32 seconds west along the said westerly limit of road allowance a distance of 107 feet more or less to the place of commencement."

It should be noted that this method of precisely describing a real estate parcel commences at a starting point known as the "Point of Commencement" and *must* completely enclose the subject property. There can be no gaps.

Identify the Property Rights Involved

It has been mentioned that a property is basically a "bundle of rights" and so value is directly proportional to the quantity and quality of rights inherent in the property. For example, a single parcel may have surface rights, mineral rights, air rights, use rights, improvement rights, lease rights, equity rights and remainder rights, each held by a different party. Or, the owner may have the fee simple interest or a life interest in the property. For this reason, the appraiser must know and state the exact interest or property rights he is required to appraise.

Interests in Land

FEE SIMPLE INTEREST

When dealing with land, the law makes a distinction between various interests in land. The first interest in land is what is known as "Fee Simple." Fee simple is the greatest interest an individual can own in land. It comes closest to the idea of complete ownership in law and when one speaks of owning land, he usually means that he holds the fee simple to it. That is, he holds it for all time, both present and future, subject only to its return to the government in the event of his dying without heirs and without having made a will granting it to someone. He may grant the whole of the fee simple away (that is, sell it); he may grant away part of his interest, keeping the rest for himself (that is, lease it); or he may grant the whole of it in various portions to different persons.

LIFE ESTATE

Another interest in land is known as the "Life Estate." This is the grant of the right to use the real property for the life of a particular person, and, upon the death of that person, the property goes to someone else. This term is commonly used in estate planning where one spouse grants to the other a life interest in the property, and upon their death the property goes to the children. Another example of a life estate occurs when a farmer sells his farm and retains the right to live in the old home on the property until his death. This type of encumbrance is particularly restrictive and certainly affects the marketability and thus value of a property.

LEASEHOLD INTEREST

Another type of interest in a property is the "Leasehold Interest." It gives to the holder of the leasehold estate (the tenant) an interest in the land for a definite period of time. The *term* of the interest is the major distinction between a "freehold" and a "leasehold" estate. A leasehold interest must be derived from a freehold interest and cannot last longer than the freehold from which it is derived.

EASEMENTS

Another limited form of interest in land is commonly known as an "Easement." An easement is a right enjoyed by one property owner over the land of another and is usually obtained for a special purpose rather than for the general use and occupation of the land. The most common type of easement is the right-of-way. Once granted, an easement attaches to the land and binds subsequent owners. They cannot interfere with the exercise of the easement.

COVENANTS

Covenants, or "Restrictive" covenants as they are sometimes called, tend to limit or control the use of the land. They are usually imposed by one land owner when deeding the land to another. These restrictive covenants always impose upon the purchaser certain limiting conditions with respect to the use of the land. (For example, they are frequently employed by oil companies to control the sale of competitive petroleum products by subsequent owners.)

Another example of this type of restriction might be in the case of the owner of a hardware store who also owns the adjacent lot and decides to sell it. He instructs his lawyer to place a restrictive covenant on the property's title which prohibits the operation of any business which would compete with his hardware store.

The following diagram illustrates the various interests in land under two main headings: **Estate in Time,** which covers interests determined according to the duration of time that the holder of the interest would have the right to exclusive possession of the land; and **Interest Less Than an Estate,** which includes interests determined according to the kind of use permitted or restricted upon the land.

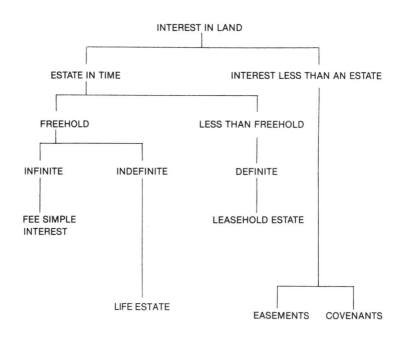

Concurrent Interests

TENANTS IN COMMON

Two or more persons may become owners of the same estate in land at the same time. They are called "concurrent" holders of the estate, whether it be a fee simple interest, life estate, or leasehold estate. In the absence of any special agreement between them, or of special terms set out in the grant by which they acquired the interest, concurrent holders are deemed to be "Tenants in Common." Each interest is an undivided interest; one tenant cannot fence off a portion of the property for his exclusive use—each is entitled to use of the whole property. Tenants in common may agree expressly to hold unequal shares. In the event of death, the interest is transferred to the beneficiary.

JOINT TENANCY

Another form of concurrent interest in land is the "Joint Tenancy."

A joint tenancy arises only when expressly created in the grant of the estate or afterwards by an express agreement between the holders of the estate. The feature which distinguishes the joint tenancy from the tenancy in common is the right of survivorship. Under the right of survivorship, the interest of a deceased joint tenant passes immediately on his or her death to the surviving tenant or tenants instead of to the heirs of the deceased tenant. Thus, if parties A, B and C own a parcel of real estate in joint tenancy, upon C's death, his interest passes to A and B, who continue to own the property as joint tenants between them. C's interest does not go to his heirs. In the event that C was married, the Family Law Reform Act requires that fifty per cent of his interest pass to the surviving spouse.

Title Systems

Title systems are methods employed to give public and official record of the ownership of interests in land. There are two systems in use in Ontario. The oldest of the two is known as the "Registry System." Under this system, the registrar records documents presented for registration and is only responsible for seeing that they are presented in the proper form. He takes no responsibility for the validity of the document. Therefore, in order to insure a proper title and ownership to real property, a lengthy and often complicated search by a solicitor is usually required.

The second title system is the "Land Titles" system (sometimes called the "Torrens" system). Under this system, the registrar is responsible for the form and validity of each document registered and, in effect, guarantees that all registered documents pertaining to each parcel of real estate are genuine.

VALUE   USAGE

Identify the Purpose and Function of the Appraisal

Another important consideration in the process of defining the problem is to establish and identify both the purpose and the function of the appraisal. While these two words are quite similar and often used interchangeably, they do have distinct and separate meanings in the world of real estate appraising.

The *purpose* of the appraisal is always to estimate a specific type of value. This is generally market value, but it could be some other type of value such as book value, insurable value, lending value, assessment value and so on.

The *function* of the appraisal refers to the *use* that will be made of the value estimate. For example, if an appraisal is required by a client who intends to sell his property, the *purpose* of the appraisal would be "to estimate market value." The *function* of the appraisal would be "to use this estimate to establish the price at which the property should be listed or sold." If the appraisal is required by a client who is not satisfied with his realty tax bill, the *purpose* of the appraisal would be "to estimate assessment value." The *function* of the appraisal would be "to determine whether there is justification for an assessment appeal."

There are five major appraisal functions which cover most basic business decisions or transactions and most appraisal assignments. They are: *USES OF APPRAISAL*

Transfer of ownership *(SALE)*

Extension of credit *(MTG.)*

Compensation for damage or loss *(EXPROPRIATION)*

Taxation *(ASSESSMENT)*

Land use studies *(CHANGE)*

Transfer of ownership involves buying, selling and exchanging of real estate, and each of these transactions requires an estimate of value.

Extension of credit usually involves mortgage lending or other financing, and an estimate of the value of the real estate is required to determine the amount of the loan.

Compensation for damage or loss covers insurance claims and expropriation.

Taxation, in its many forms, includes municipal assessment for real estate taxes and income tax on capital gains.

Land use studies or feasibility studies are often carried out for developers or investors contemplating some different form of use for a particular parcel of land and this usually involves an estimate of value under different programs of development.

In view of the different purposes and the many functions for which an appraisal may be required, it is essential that these be established at the very beginning of the assignment. Furthermore, both the purpose and the function should be stated in the appraisal report to clarify the appraisal problem and ensure that there will be no misunderstanding as to the type of value being appraised.

Define the Type of Value Required

Once the purpose of the appraisal has been stated explicitly, the appraiser can summarize his objectives by clearly defining the value concept to be applied.

As mentioned earlier, value is a word of many meanings and even a specific type of value may be subject to different interpretations. A property can have more than one value at the same time but it has only one market value or other *specific* value as of a given date.

The market value of the property is an estimate of its probable selling price based on the past behaviour of typical purchasers. The value for insurance purposes, at the same date, is based on reproduction cost of a building (usually not including its foundations) but less depreciation. The value in use, at the same date, could involve an item such as a large area within a special use structure controlled as to humidity, temperature and absence of dust, which is vitally necessary for the manufacture of one of the owner's products. This latter item could not represent its full value to a prospective purchaser who has no use for it.

Because confusion about the type of assignment can arise, in each instance the definition of value should be given in full by the appraiser. This will prevent the possibility of uninformed people misinterpreting the exact meaning of certain terms commonly used by appraisers and will ensure that there will be no misunderstanding as to the type of value required, versus that which is being appraised and reported.

If the value estimate is to be based on a special set or alternate sets of circumstances, these conditions should be stated with the definition of value.

Identify the Date of the Appraisal

The final consideration in defining the problem is to identify the date of appraisal. Every estimate of value is valid only under specific market conditions. This applies whether it is market value, insurable value, investment value, lending value, or any other specific value that is to be estimated. Value is the result of the interaction of the forces of market supply and demand. When these conditions change, so will the value estimate based upon them. Therefore, every appraisal must be made as of a specific date to identify the prevailing market forces and conditions in terms of which value is estimated. This is the *effective* date of the appraisal, often referred to as "the date on which the appraisal applies," or the "as of" date.

Most value estimates for the transfer of ownership or for the extension of credit are required as of the current date. The character of the data and the time and effort involved usually follow a familiar pattern. They concern conditions that can be observed at the time the valuation is made.

In many cases, however, a valuation is required as of some date in the past. Such valuations may require retrospective estimates as of dates varying from months to years earlier. Retrospective appraisals may be required for probating a will and settling an estate. In this case, the effective date would be the date of the demise of the owner. The effective date of an appraisal to settle a fire insurance claim will, in all likelihood, be the date on which the fire occurred. In appraising for expropriation, the effective date will be governed by the particular expropriation act, but is usually the date of the taking or registration of the expropriation.

An appraisal for capital gains taxation is another type of retroactive appraisal. When this is the function of the appraisal, the appraiser will have to estimate the value of the property "as of" December 31st, 1971 and its current market value at the time of sale to establish the amount of capital gain. This type of retroactive appraising presents some unique difficulties and requires a very analytical approach in the valuation process. The problem areas specifically are:

The subject property may have been remodelled or renovated, or other improvements may have been completed since 1971. The property being inspected today for purposes of estimating value could have appeared drastically different in 1971.

The comparables being inspected today may also have received substantial alterations since they sold in the 1971-72 time period. It is therefore important to carefully question reliable sources in order to determine exactly what changes have taken place over the years.

As evidenced by the preceding examples, certain events may very well dictate what the effective date of the appraisal should be. However, in practice the effective date of the appraisal usually comes from the client. It is important to obtain this information at the very beginning of the assignment because it establishes the market conditions under which the value is to be estimated. Finally, it is most important that the effective date be clearly recorded in the appraisal report. An appraiser can be very embarrassed by failure to put a date on the estimate if that estimate is used a year, three years or five years later.

Summary

The first step in the appraisal process involves a precise understanding of the problem. This consists of:

1. A proper identification of the property being appraised, usually by its municipal address, and a legal description, either by lot and plan number or by metes and bounds, so that the boundaries of the property can be identified.

2. Ascertaining the property rights to be appraised, for example, whether the owner has a fee simple interest or a lesser interest such as a leasehold interest.

3. Determining the purpose of the appraisal, that is, the type of value to be estimated; also, the function of the appraisal—the use that the specific value will serve once it is communicated to the client.

4. Defining the specific type of value. For example, if market value is the specific type of value required, then the definition of market value should be spelled out in writing.

5. Stating the effective date of the appraisal, that is, the date on which the value estimate applies.

Chapter 2

Step Two
Preliminary Survey and Appraisal Plan

Preliminary Survey

The preliminary survey is the first phase of the field work and involves a "windshield inspection" of the neighbourhood and the property being appraised. This initial inspection will provide the appraiser with the necessary information to determine the five main factors that are considered in making a preliminary survey. These are:

Determine Highest and Best Use — *LEGAL – ZONING*
PHYSICAL – BLDG. CODE
Determine type of data needed *MARKET – DEMAND*
ECONOMIC – PROFIT
※ Determine if additional help is required

Determine the approaches to be used

Determine work involved; set fee; obtain commitment.

Determine Highest and Best Use *A*

In appraisal practice, the concept of highest and best use represents the premise upon which value is based. In an earlier chapter of this text, the principle of highest and best use was defined as "that use which, at the time of the appraisal, is most likely to produce the greatest net return to the land, in money or amenities, over a given period of time."

This definition applies specifically to the highest and best use of the land. It is to be recognized that in cases where a site has existing improvements on it, the highest and best use may very well be determined to be different from the existing use. The existing use will continue, however, unless and until land value in its highest and best use exceeds the total value of the property in its existing use. Consequently, in estimating market value, the appraiser must consider not only the use to which the property is being put at the time, but also the likely uses to which it is adapted and for which it is capable of being used in the reasonably foreseeable future. Purely speculative future uses may not be considered.

Since owners have a natural tendency to utilize their property as advantageously as possible, and since economic pressures usually dictate the optimum or most profitable use, the highest and best use of a property will most often be its present use. But this is not always the case. There are instances where owners, for various reasons, do not utilize their property at its highest and best use, at least as the term is used here in the appraisal sense. This is especially true in rapidly expanding areas and along major new highways. Today we live in a dynamic and changing society. The passage of time often brings about radical changes in optimum land usage. Rural areas become housing developments; residential properties yield to commercial and industrial expansion. Consequently, the use to which a parcel of real estate is being put at any given time may no longer constitute its highest and best use. The classic example of this is the case of the farm located reasonably close to a city. At some point in time the farm acreage may become more valuable as a residential subdivision site than as a farm. If the appraiser concludes that the highest and best use of a farm property would be as a site for a subdivision, then he should appraise the property as a potential subdivision site rather than as a farm.

Before basing a value estimate on a use other than its existing use, the appraiser must first be convinced of three things:

That the property is *physically* adaptable to the other use

That an actual *demand* exists for the other use sufficient to enhance the market value

That the property is *available* for such other use in that it would not be in violation of existing zoning by-laws or private deed restrictions.

The appraiser may consider a use which is presently prohibited by the zoning by-laws *if* there is good reason and evidence to believe that a change in the zoning by-law allowing that particular use is *probable*, not simply possible, and that the change is imminent.

Change in the highest and best use of a property usually comes about gradually, and usually after it has benefited from its existing use for a considerable period of time. There are instances, however, when a change in the highest and best use can occur quite suddenly, as, for example, following a zoning change.

Determine Type of Data Needed

The type and quantity of data that will be required, gathered and analyzed will depend a great deal on the purpose and function of the appraisal, and more particularly on the type of property that is being appraised. Data pertinent to the appraisal of a single-family residential property differs considerably from data assembled to appraise a shopping centre or an industrial property. Furthermore, as might be expected, it requires considerably more information to appraise a hotel than a residential single-family dwelling.

Appraisal data includes all information that will assist the appraiser in making an estimate of value. It consists of:

> *General* data on economic, political, social and physical factors, forces and trends in the region, city and neighbourhood, and ...

> *Specific* data relating to the property itself, the site, the title, the improvements and specific information on comparable properties. The type of specific data will depend on the type of property being appraised and also on the techniques or approaches used in estimating its value.

Determine if Additional Help is Required

Generally speaking, the appraiser can cope with most appraisal assignments without the need of outside assistance. Occasionally, however, some of the data may be highly technical in nature, requiring the appraiser to rely on the services of other experts. Engineers are often used in construction analysis. Surveyors establish boundaries and contours. Title searchers examine public records. Economists provide economic background analysis. Lawyers are engaged to render legal opinion as to title or ownership. Quantity surveyors are hired to cost buildings and other improvements. Landscape architects estimate the value of trees and shrubbery. Agricultural experts render reports on soil conditions and fertility, water flows and similar factors. Planners assist in determining highest and best use of land. The use of such experts is a necessary step if the appraiser is to have accurate data bearing on appraisal assignments.

If any such specialists are to be engaged by the appraiser to assist in the appraisal assignment, agreement must be reached with respect to the extent of their involvement; the time schedule within which their report must be submitted, and the cost of their service.

Determine the Approaches to be Used

Having made a preliminary inspection of the property, even if it is only a casual look at the exterior of the property, the experienced appraiser can usually arrive at some conclusion as to the approaches that would be used to estimate its value.

The three recognized approaches are the **Cost Approach**, the **Income Approach** and the **Direct Sales Comparison Approach**. All three approaches will not necessarily be pertinent in every appraisal. Again, the nature of the property will usually dictate the most relevant approach. Another significant factor is the amount of information available to process each approach.

Determine Work Involved; Set Fee; Obtain Commitment

Based on the factors previously considered in the preliminary survey, that is, determining the data needed; determining what additional assistance may be required; and determining which approaches are to be used, the appraiser can determine the amount of work that will be involved and the amount of time that will be required to complete the appraisal assignment.

The next step is to establish the fee. The appraiser usually finds it necessary to quote a fee before receiving a firm commitment to proceed with the appraisal. The fee is customarily a figure charged on a rate per hour or per day based on ability, integrity and experience. In order to set the fee, the appraiser usually considers the time involved, possible cash outlays, degree of experience involved and whether outside experts must be hired.

It is good business practice to get a written commitment from your client *prior* to commencing work. There have been instances where appraisal fees were not collected simply because of a misunderstanding between the appraiser and client. Such problems are effectively eliminated by clear, concise, written instructions from the client. A brief letter outlining the important details may follow the following format:

Dear Mr. _____

The purpose of this letter is to confirm my telephone request that you appraise the property located at . . . . . . for the purpose of estimating the building value only. It is understood that this value estimate will be used as a basis for arranging adequate insurance coverage. I agree to pay you the amount of . . . . . . as soon as I receive your report. It is understood that this report will be received by . . . . . .

Yours truly,

This letter, prepared by the appraiser, should be typed in duplicate and forwarded to the client. All the client must do now is to sign one for the appraiser's files and retain the duplicate for his own records. This system ensures harmony of understanding right through to the presentation of the valuation report.

The Appraisal Plan

When the preliminary survey has been completed and agreement reached with the client, the actual appraisal work commences. One of the most effective means of beginning is to prepare a complete outline of the report, including tentative lists of tables, charts, diagrams and maps which will be needed and headings for the principal sections and subsections of the report. Such an outline permits the intelligent and orderly assemblage of data and the judicious allocation of time to the various steps involved.

Correct scheduling and planning of the appraisal will yield numerous advantages. A clear and definite understanding of the exact nature of the work to be done by the appraiser and that which is to be done by others will expedite the efficient handling of the assignment.

Once the outline is completed the work of filling in the report begins. As the data are collected, they can be fitted into this outline readily, so that subsequent report writing is facilitated.

Summary

The preliminary survey involves a cursory inspection of the neighbourhood and the subject site to evaluate the extent of the problem to be solved and to acquire some idea of the amount of work involved. This will require consideration of the highest and best use of the property; determination of the quantity and type of data that will be required to solve the problem; whether any outside assistance will be required; the likely approach to be used; and finally, agreement with the client concerning the appraisal fee.

When authority has been granted to proceed with the appraisal, a well organized appraiser commences his work by making a preliminary plan of the appraisal report he will present.

Chapter 3

Step Three
Data Collection and Analysis

It was mentioned in the preceding chapter that the appraiser, when conducting the preliminary survey, would endeavour to determine the type of data necessary, significant and pertinent to the solution of the particular appraisal problem. The nature and extent of this information would depend largely on the type of property being appraised and also on the purpose and function of the appraisal. These data usually comprise two broad classifications: **General Data**, such as data on economic, political, social and physical forces affecting real estate values in the region and including information regarding trends in the immediate neighbourhood; and **Specific Data** relating to the subject property and the specific comparables used in the appraisal. Specific data include such facts as lot size, taxes, building size, room size, title information such as easements, etc. The type of specific data will depend upon the method, technique or approaches to value to be employed. If the property is residential in nature it is unlikely that income data on commercial properties will be of any assistance.

General Data

Because of its fixed location, real estate is a creature of its environment and its use and value is very much influenced by external factors and forces resulting from national and regional trends but even more directly by local or neighbourhood trends. The area of investigation, therefore, extends inward from the outermost fringe of the research area to the immediate area in which the subject is located (see **Figure 2**).

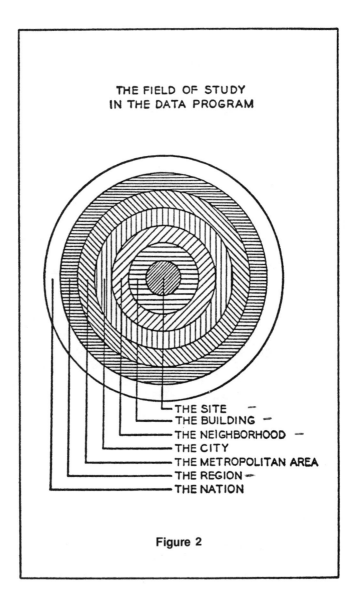

THE FIELD OF STUDY
IN THE DATA PROGRAM

THE SITE
THE BUILDING
THE NEIGHBORHOOD
THE CITY
THE METROPOLITAN AREA
THE REGION
THE NATION

Figure 2

Trends

Under the category of general data, a discussion of regional and local trends is appropriate, so that the appraiser will be in an excellent position to forecast, with some degree of confidence, what the probable future prospects of the local area will be. For example, in estimating the value of a tri-plex property it is important for the appraiser to know what competition exists for this type of accommodation in the neighbourhood. The appraiser must also be conversant with rental rates and sale price trends for multi-family units. Possibly there is a scarcity of this type of property and accordingly this factor will influence values.

It is important to note that it is the *trends* that are critical and not the static circumstances of the moment. Remember, a purchaser of this type of property will not only consider the property in its present state but will also think in terms of what he can derive from it in the future. While it is acknowledged that past trends are no guarantee of the future, they nevertheless, if properly interpreted, provide a valuable guide.

A "trend" is defined as a series of related changes brought about by a chain of causes and effects. It has four distinct features:

Time

Direction

Cause

Effect

It is not enough to know that changes have, and are taking place. It is essential to find out the direction of the trend and its limit so that it may be properly analyzed regarding possible future effects on property values.

It is very helpful to provide visual evidence in the form of a graph or chart for purposes of assisting the reader in identifying the time and direction of trends. Not only is such visual evidence easily interpreted, it also provides strong support for value conclusions and analyses which may have been previously referred to in the valuation report.

There can be many variations of this graphic type of reporting and graphs may be used to illustrate any one of many interesting conclusions. For instance, Figures 3 and 4 are excerpts from "Toronto Real Estate Board—M.L.S. Statistics" (modified), showing "smoothed" average sales prices for all houses sold through M.L.S. The information given in Figures 3 and 4 is identical, however, the graphic illustration more clearly and simply demonstrates the "time and direction" of the

Figure 3

Smoothed Monthly Average Prices — Toronto MLS Average House Prices

	1977	1978	1979	1980	1981	1982	1983	1984	1985	1986	1987
Jan	62448	64993	68925	72064	77346	97412	98554	99265	103822	118644	165799
Feb	63070	65167	68744	73067	79065	96379	102883	100845	105339	122596	175220
Mar	63785	65704	69445	73220	82211	95185	103241	102373	106082	127339	
Apr	64697	66591	71267	74364	87365	94878	102603	103336	107087	131601	
May	65342	67672	72365	76376	93552	96290	103232	103736	108488	134187	
June	65518	68184	72314	77161	99442	96878	103441	103048	108433	137051	
July	65303	68505	72016	76936	102055	95571	102705	102224	108397	139976	
Aug	64386	68432	71356	76603	100127	94258	100547	101633	108959	142638	
Sept	64023	67981	70774	76252	97662	93673	99358	101527	109887	147048	
Oct	64563	67841	70430	76394	97927	94917	100045	102206	112191	152784	
Nov	65038	67892	69983	76651	99063	96212	100412	102681	114293	158050	
Dec	65193	68454	70518	76606	98606	95922	99519	102894	115799	161577	

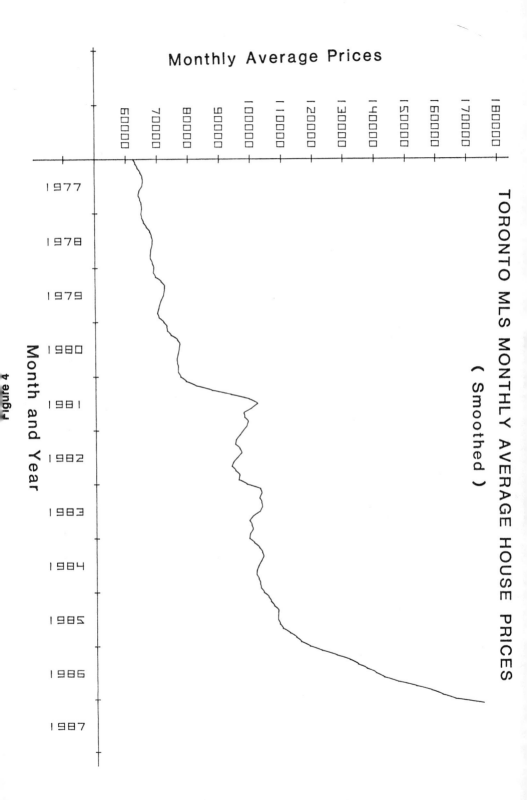

Monthly Average Prices

Month and Year

Figure 4

TORONTO MLS MONTHLY AVERAGE HOUSE PRICES

(Smoothed)

60000
70000
80000
90000
100000
110000
120000
130000
140000
150000
160000
170000
180000

1977
1978
1979
1980
1981
1982
1983
1984
1985
1986
1987

trend. In addition, the graph gives an historic base from which reasonable assumptions for the immediate future can be made: e.g. prices appear to have stabilized from mid-1974 to the end of 1980 compared to the rapid rise experienced in 1973. The graph also depicts the phenomenal increase in house prices experienced in Metropolitan Toronto in the first seven months of 1981, followed by a gradual decline thereafter.

The foregoing examples illustrate how trends can be measured and used as a tool in the appraisal process.

Some other regional or local trends that are of importance and concern to the appraiser in the analysis and evaluation of external market forces might include:

Regional or local economy

Population growth or decline

Purchasing power

General price levels

Building cycles

Building costs

Real estate taxes

Interest rates

Government controls

Urban renewal

Neighbourhood Analysis

DEFINITION OF A NEIGHBOURHOOD — *GEOGRAPHIC LOCATION*
GROUPED AROUND A KEY FOCAL POINT, OR BOUNDED BY SIMILAR
A neighbourhood is a division of a city, town or community. It is *FEATUR* *OR* a segment within a larger unit, that is, the community to which it belongs. *DRAWN* It is a grouping of individuals for similar reasons, whether they be *TOGETHE* for commercial, industrial, residential, cultural or civic reasons. It is *BY* shaped and molded by social, economic, civic and physical factors and *SIMILAR* any fluctuation in these broad basic factors will modify its character. *REASONS.*

NEIGHBOURHOOD AGE CYCLE — *DETERMINES VALUE*

An important consideration in the valuation process is the determination of a neighbourhood's age cycle position. Every neighbourhood goes through a complete life cycle that has three distinct stages: **growth, stability** and **decline.**

The first stage in the cycle, known as the period of growth, is the development period when the neighbourhood gains public favour and acceptance. The second stage is stability when the area is completely built up and values tend to be at their highest. The last and final stage of the cycle is that of decline when the buildings pass the prime of their economic life. It should be noted that neighbourhoods in their final stage quite often revert back to the stage of stability as a result of programs of rehabilitation or urban renewal. This cyclical economic behaviour may repeat itself until finally the neighbourhood reaches a status of blight and prospective slum conditions.

NEIGHBOURHOOD BOUNDARIES

While a neighbourhood is a neighbourhood mainly because of its character, and while it may have definite boundaries, it is not an isolated section; it is only a segment of the whole and is influenced by the sector encompassing it. Each neighbourhood in a city, town or village, is dependent on all the other neighbourhoods in its community.

Similarly, in a metropolitan area, the different municipalities within the metropolitan area are dependent on all the other municipalities within that area.

A neighbourhood has a distinct identity. There are several factors that set it apart from surrounding areas and which make it easy to delineate. These are:

Natural Boundaries: rivers, lakes, hills, mountains, ravines, etc.

Political Boundaries: municipal boundaries or city limits, land use or zoning change, school area, etc.

Man-made Boundaries: railroad tracks, major highways or roads, hydro right-of-ways, etc.

FACTORS OR FORCES AFFECTING NEIGHBOURHOOD ~ PEPS
(PHYSICAL, ECONOMICAL, POLITICAL, SOCIAL)

Once the neighbourhood has been delineated and identified, the appraiser's next task is to consider the economic, social, political and physical factors and forces at work within the neighbourhood which influence both property values and changes in these values.

Occupant Analysis
owners, renters
Vacancies?

The data and type of analysis employed must be pertinent to the specific appraisal problem at hand. The mere listing of data, factors or forces influencing value is simply not enough. The data must be analyzed and interpreted. The appraiser must show *how* and *why* these items do influence the value of the subject property. The following is a list of such data that must be considered:

zoning & land use
transformation
shopping
churches
schools/parks
distance to industry/employment

Economic

Economic reason for the existence of the neighbourhood and future prospects.

Wage levels and job opportunities.

Interest rates and lender's attitude to the particular area.

Average prices of properties in the area.

Value of retail trade.

Trend of home ownership as opposed to residential tenancy and vacancy rates.

Economic transition—growth, stability, decline.

Social

Population, its growth, age and make-up.

Family size and formation.

Existence of amenities such as recreation and educational facilities.

The availability, location and distance to shopping centres and places of employment.

Political

Type and effectiveness of local government.

Local government attitudes towards taxes, assessments, planning and zoning.

Attitude towards industry and other real estate development.

Type of political structure and stability of government.

Physical

Location of city in relation to regional markets and geographical features.

Location of neighbourhood relative to city centre and employment areas.

Street layouts and subdivision system.

Transportation facilities.

Physical beauty, including topography and landscape.

Climatic features, such as average temperatures and precipitation.

Existence of undesirable elements such as: location in relation to incompatible land uses and other detrimental geographical features.

Sources of General Data

The neighbourhood analysis cannot be carried out without having good, reliable and accurate data which have been verified at the source whenever possible.

Usually, appraisers are reasonably familiar with the neighbourhood in the city or community in which they work. The knowledge of a neighbourhood required to properly value real estate located there, should be almost second nature to them. The first and most obvious source to which appraisers should turn for obtaining neighbourhood data is their own files. Once these are developed and organized systematically, the appraiser will have a wealth of general data available.

Other sources of general data include local real estate offices, local businessmen, Chamber of Commerce, publications on building permits issued, neighbours, etc.

Analyzing the Low Density Residential Neighbourhood

Residential property appraisal probably constitutes the greatest volume of work for most appraisers. Many of the factors affecting residential property value are difficult to measure because single family homes are generally purchased on the basis of the enjoyment and benefits of ownership, as opposed to the economic return being obtained from ownership. The typical buyer is most concerned with the intangible occupational rights of ownership, whereas the income producing capabilities of the home are probably of marginal consideration. The appraiser should know what neighbourhood factors to look for as well as their effect on the desirability and enhancement of residential property values. Figure 5 is a typical residential neighbourhood data form.

PHYSICAL

It has been said that the three most important factors affecting value of any type of property are location, location and location! This holds particularly true for residential properties, and all other factors are related to location. If a single family home is poorly located, this will generally tend to offset all the other beneficial factors affecting value. In addition to location, the appraiser should consider: public transportation, parks, schools, churches, retail and service outlets, topography and landscape, availability and quality of utilities, and nuisances or hazards such as smoke, noise, pollution and heavy traffic.

ECONOMIC

The appraiser should be aware of: stability of uses, property values, income and population, vacancies, new construction, personal and family income levels, degree of maintenance (pride of ownership), stage in the neighbourhood's life, vacant land, mortgage lending policies, interest rates, sales price trends, and rate of turnover.

POLITICAL OR GOVERNMENTAL

The appraiser should be aware of the legal factors which affect low density residential values, some of which are: zoning regulations and building codes, property taxes and local improvement taxes, official plans, deed restrictions.

SOCIAL

Significant social factors which the appraiser should consider are: population trends with respect to growth or decline, population movement, trends to larger or smaller family sizes, harmony or lack of harmony of ethnic or economic groupings, educational attitudes, prestige or lack thereof, crime rates, age groupings, and population densities.

Analyzing the Apartment Neighbourhood

In a general way those factors that are necessary to the desirability of a residential neighbourhood must also be present in an apartment district, but there is a difference in the stress given them. The more important factors in an apartment location are:

Transportation. Apartments should be located where public transportation is fast and convenient.

Major Thoroughfares. Major traffic arteries should be nearby and apartment tenants should not have to pass through otherwise quiet residential areas to get to major arteries.

Services. There must be convenience to shopping centres, schools, churches and the like.

Amenities and Recreational Facilities (Physical). The proximity of an apartment location to a river, parks, playgrounds or other pleasant features can add to the desirability of the location and reduce the effects of possible future competition in the area.

Figure 5

Neighbourhood Data Form

1. BOUNDARIES:
   NORTH _____ SOUTH _____ EAST _____ WEST _____
2. LIFE CYCLE OF NEIGHBOURHOOD: DEVELOPMENT ☐ EQUILIBRIUM ☐ DECLINE ☐
3. LAND VALUE TREND: UPWARD ☐ DOWNWARD ☐ STABLE ☐ RATE PER YEAR _____ %
4. ECONOMIC & POLITICAL FACTORS:
   - ZONING _____ PERCENT BUILT UP _____
   - PRICE RANGE OF TYPICAL PROPERTIES: FROM $_____ TO $ _____
   - PREDOMINANT TYPE BLDG: _____ TYPICAL AGE: _____
   - OWNER OCCUPANCY PERCENTAGE _____ RENTAL OCCUPANCY PERCENTAGE_____
   - MARKETABILITY: GOOD ☐ FAIR ☐ POOR ☐
5. UTILITIES:
   - ELECTRICITY ☐   - GAS ☐
   - WATER ☐   - TELEPHONE ☐
   - SEWERAGE ☐   - SIDEWALK ☐
   - STREET SURFACING ☐
6. DEED RESTRICTIONS: YES ☐ NO ☐ SPECIFY _____
7. SPECIAL ASSESSMENTS: OUTSTANDING _____ EXPECTED_____
8. TAX RATE _____
   COMPARISON TO SIMILAR PROPERTIES IN COMPETING NEIGHBOURHOODS:
   HIGH ☐ LOW ☐ SAME ☐
9. DISTANCE FROM SCHOOLS: _____
10. DISTANCE FROM CHURCHES OR SYNAGOGUES: _____
11. DISTANCE FROM SHOPPING-FACILITIES: _____
12. PUBLIC TRANSPORTATION (Specify type): _____
    FREQUENCY OF SERVICE _____
    DISTANCE FROM NEIGHBOURHOOD TO BOARDING POINT _____
    DISTANCE FROM NEIGHBOURHOOD TO CENTRAL BUSINESS DISTRICT _____
    TIME TO REACH CENTRAL BUSINESS AREA _____
13. TYPES OF SERVICES OFFERED IN THE NEIGHBOURHOOD:
    - POLICE AND FIRE PROTECTION ☐   - DELIVERY SERVICES ☐
    - GARBAGE COLLECTION ☐   - OTHERS (specify) _____
14. DISTANCE FROM RECREATIONAL & CULTURAL AREAS
    (Parks, playgrounds, theaters, libraries, bowling alleys, etc.)_____
15. SPECIAL TRAFFIC PROBLEMS _____
16. HAZARDS (airport, gas or oil storage, etc.) _____
17. NUISANCES (noise, smoke, odors, etc.) _____
18. SOCIAL AND ECONOMIC BACKGROUND OF RESIDENTS:
    - TYPICAL FAMILY INCOME $ _____ TO $ _____
    - PREDOMINANT ETHNIC GROUP _____
    - PREDOMINANT RELIGIOUS GROUP _____
    - PREDOMINANT OCCUPATIONS OF RESIDENTS _____
      _____
    - AVERAGE FAMILY SIZE _____

Vacancies. Short-run apartment vacancies, resulting from boom construction conditions, should be assessed in conjunction with the possible future market for apartment units in a neighbourhood. Important factors include the increasing population of a city, the swelling in population of certain age groups, the vacant land in the area suitable for future apartment construction and others of a like nature. The appraisal of an apartment should be concerned with possible long-term vacancies, over the future economic life of the building, and not just with short-term vacancy ratios that will fluctuate over the years. In most cities, Canada Mortgage and Housing Corporation publishes the results of its vacancy surveys in different neighbourhoods, as prepared from time to time.

Analyzing the Commercial Area

In dealing with commercial areas, the appraiser must consider some different factors:

The **Extent, Population, Incomes** and **Demand** of the trading area.

Major Traffic Thoroughfares. The commercial neighbourhood must have ready access from the surrounding residential districts.

Parking Facilities. These must be ample and easy to find.

Competition from Other Areas. The pull of competition from other neighbourhoods must be analyzed for its effect on the area being evaluated.

Compatibility of Uses. The degree of compatibility between the commercial uses in a neighbourhood should be considered. In the case of retail stores, for example, certain lines of merchandise such as food, drugs, hardware, variety items and so forth are compatible and act together to draw trade to a neighbourhood.

Direction of Growth. The 100% location should be established from where the trends of growth can be defined.

Vacancies. Vacancies of both buildings and land should be noted.

Analyzing the Industrial Area

The main factors, in addition to those already enumerated, are:

Labour Pool. There must be an ample supply of skilled workers within easy commuting distance.

Services. Convenient access to major highways and truck routes is important. Rail service and the possibility of interswitching privileges between the main railway companies can be a necessary condition for many industries, and, of course, roads, utilities, police, fire and other services must be analyzed.

Materials. If raw materials are needed in the manufacture of certain items in the neighbourhood, they must be readily accessible to the district.

Analyzing the Farm Area

The farm appraiser is concerned with many of the factors mentioned previously, plus a host of others, including:

Distance to market.

Types of soils and crops grown.

Community life of the farmers.

Typical farm units; their size and operations.

Services, including roads, power, mail delivery, school transportation and so forth.

Pressure for urbanization.

In a city it is comparatively easy to determine neighbourhoods by the grouping together of people for different reasons. These neighbourhoods are generally defined by more-or-less natural boundaries, although they can infringe on one another. In rural areas neighbourhoods may be harder to discern, but like city districts they may infringe on one another.

Specific Data

This is the information to be gathered with respect to the subject site, the improvements on and to the site, and specific information on comparable properties being used in arriving at an estimate of value of the subject property.

Site Versus Land

Land is unimproved by man. It consists of the surface of the earth, suprasurface air space, and subsurface area. It is usually referred to as "raw acreage," "raw land" or "unimproved land." _Site_, on the other hand, is a parcel of land which has been subdivided and serviced to some degree so that it can be utilized for the purpose for which it is intended, usually as a building site. Generally speaking, it will have been cleared; graded for drainage; provided with access to a street or road; provided with storm and sanitary sewers, and gas, water, electricity and telephone service; and arrangements made so that it is not legally constrained from being put to its intended use.

Data Required for Site Analysis and Valuation

The data to be gathered must be pertinent to the requirements of both the proposed use of the site and its valuation. These data must provide the basis for the site analysis and are usually classified under four main headings, as described below.

Physical Factors: site dimensions (frontage, depth, width, shape, area), soils, topography, plottage, excess land and assembly, climatic conditions, services and utilities, road and street patterns, landscaping, etc.

Locational Factors: land use pattern, access, corner influences, hazards and nuisances, etc.

Legal-Governmental Factors: legal description, title data, easements, zoning, assessment and taxes, private restrictions, etc.

Economic Factors: prices of comparable sites, tax burden, utility costs, service costs, etc.

Sources of Specific Data ← REGISTRY OFFICE

One of the most important contributory factors in the process of data collection, especially the information pertaining directly to the physical attributes of the site and the improvements, is the actual inspection of the property. The physical on-site inspection will provide the appraiser with factual data required for the valuation.

Another very important source of specific data, especially that information dealing with the legal-governmental factors, is the municipal office or city hall and the Registry or Land Titles Office.

Real estate offices are a valuable source of data regarding listings and sales and in many cases information of a "motivational" nature regarding the circumstances of an individual sale. Direct interviews with the participants involved in the sale are usually the most revealing and informative sources however, particularly when you wish to fully understand the reasons why a property sold for the price that it did. Mortgage and loan offices will provide data regarding prevailing interest rates, a very important consideration in today's market place. Newspapers should be consulted regularly, as in many instances major developments are first made public through the news media. Government offices are another good source, particularly of specialized information, e.g. Revenue Canada regarding taxation implications on real estate, etc.

The appraiser will also find that the office of a local real estate appraiser could be an excellent source of data. These appraisers spend a great deal of time and money maintaining comprehensive data banks for the purpose of carrying on their daily business. Specific types of information to be found in these offices may include data on construction costs, land sales data, rental information and other relevant real estate data. Generally speaking, appraisers will fully cooperate with other appraisers in the exchange of this type of information.

PLOTTAGE - VALUE ↑
EXCESS LAND - UTILITY ↓
ASSEMBLAGE -

The Site Analysis — SIZE, SHAPE, LOCATION - DATA REQD.

A comprehensive site analysis is basic to the valuation of any site. Characteristic uniformity may not prevail in all locations of the neighbourhood. Sites differ in locational, physical, legal and economic attributes, all of which must be analyzed separately. Before the highest and best use of the site can be estimated and subsequently valued, the major forces affecting its value must be analyzed through regional and neighbourhood data. Conclusions drawn from the neighbourhood analysis are related to conclusions drawn from the site analysis, from which a highest and best use is estimated.

Highest and Best Use

The first step in the valuation of a site is to arrive at an estimate of its highest and best use. The highest and best use of any particular site is usually defined as *that use which, at the time of appraisal, is most likely to produce the greatest net return, in money or amenities over a given period of time.*

LEGAL - ZONING
PHYSICAL - CONFORMITY
ECONOMICAL - FEE

IMPROVED SITES   MARKET -

The existing use of a given parcel of land is usually the highest and best use, since economic pressures dictate the use. If the existing use is the highest and best use, it should:

conform to the existing zoning regulations or be a legal non-conforming use;

be in reasonable conformity with its surroundings;

pay the owner to continue in that use, as long as the buildings contribute something to the total property value in excess of the value of the vacant site.

When the appraiser is convinced that the existing use is not the highest and best use of the site, the existing use must be ignored in the site valuation.

Often, a building will contribute very little, if anything, to the overall property value. Visualize a small bungalow located on a busy, commercially developed street. A drug store is located on one side of this bungalow and a lawyer's office on the other side. During the previous several years this area has been changing from primarily residential to commercial use. In such a case it is clear that the value of the property is primarily in the land. Very likely a purchaser of this property will develop it to some other use which would conform to the other properties in the immediate area. It is in such a circumstance as this that the appraiser must ignore the existing use and contemplate the higher and better use in arriving at a market value listing price.

UNIMPROVED SITES

The highest and best use of an unimproved site is usually dictated by the zoning by-laws governing the particular site in question. In some cases, however, a different type of use might appear to be the highest and best use. Examples of this are residential lots in close proximity to expanding commercial areas, or so located that there is a reasonable probability of rezoning to a higher residential density.

If the highest and best use is estimated to be a use which is not permitted by existing zoning regulations, there must be ample evidence that the probability of a change in regulations is reasonably certain and imminent. There must be a strong demand for such use.

Factors in Site Analysis

In arriving at an estimate of the highest and best use of a particular site and further analyzing the site for valuation purposes, the appraiser must identify the anticipated needs and requirements of proposed users, and must match these needs and requirements with the characteristics of the site in terms of the factors discussed below.

Physical Factors

This part of the analysis deals with forces pertinent to the physical utility of the site. These on-site factors fall within the boundaries of the site itself and together from the basis of its utility and comparability with other sites. The immobility of the site subjects it's value entirely to the influences of its particular utility, location factors and neighbourhood forces.

SITE DIMENSIONS

Frontage. Frontage is that side of a site which abuts a public street or highway. It is the basis for a value unit as well as being an important factor in determining accessibility and prominence.

Depth. Depth is the distance between the front and rear lot lines.

Width. Width is the distance between the side lines of a lot. The depth and width of a lot may be consistent or it may vary depending upon its shape.

Shape. The shape of a site is its form, determined by the frontage, depth and width. Shape largely determines utility and desirability.

Area. Area is the quantum of space provided by a site resulting from the product of its dimensions.

Frontage, depth, width, shape and area together create the ultimate desire, utility and value of any site. Zoning by-laws often require a minimum frontage and area for certain uses. Frontage and area form the basis for value units and comparability with other sites. **N.B. When making reference to the frontage and depth of sites, the frontage measurement is always shown first.**

Within a given neighbourhood, it is usual for similar sites to conform to a specific or general size and standard regarding frontage, depth and area. Modern subdivisions with cul-de-sacs and curved streets very often cause a variance in site frontage and depth but attempt to maintain similar site areas. In such cases the frontage value may not be a good unit of comparison whereas the area indicator may be. Standard sites of a particular use will have comparable frontage, depth and area to provide the desired utility and balance for the improvement. Often, sites will vary in frontage and depth yet sell at a similar price because of their equivalent utility.

When frontage and depth are greater than the standard for the area, the excess land seldom contributes proportionate value except for specialized land uses where the land is purchased on a unit area basis. An example of this is the price paid and the comparability between a standard subdivision site and a one hectare site both of which are legally limited to one single family residence. The hectare site may provide many times the area yet sell for about the same or a little more than the subdivision site. It is most important, therefore, when comparing sites by either a front metre or square metre rate, that all sites be reasonably comparable in both frontage and depth.

SOILS

The soils of a given site may be sandy, clay, rock or silt. The type of soil found on a site will affect its value through site preparation and cost of site development. Low-lying sites may require fill or shoring; rocky sites may require blasting; silty sites may require pilings; hardpan sites may require extra costs for landscaping; heavy clay may require additional cost for septic tile beds, where no sewers are available and septic tank systems are required. Since the value of a site in contribution to a completed property depends on its development cost, soil type is of basic importance in site analysis. In certain instances, it may be desirable to secure soil tests.

PLOTTAGE, EXCESS LAND AND ASSEMBLAGE

Plottage is a value increment resulting from the assembly of two or more smaller sites when the combined utility is proportionately greater than the sum of the individual utilities. For example, five 5 metre sites in a commercial strip may be worth $1,500 per front metre if sold separately. However, combined, the 25 metre lot provides greater flexibility and utility for a block of stores and may be worth $2,250 per front metre. As such, a plottage increment of $750 per front metre is gained through the assembly. For plottage to apply, the character and use of the land must change so that the value of the whole exceeds the sum of its parts.

Excess land results from a site being larger than standard where the additional size does not provide proportional utility. A good example of this is found with various size single family residential sites. The going rate for a standard size lot measuring 15 metres by 30 metres (approximately 50 feet by 100 feet) may be $24,000. This reflects unit value rates of $1,600 per front metre, or $53.33 per square metre (Approximately $480 per front foot and $4.80 per square foot.) By comparison, a larger site, say 18 metres by 45 metres (approximately 59 feet by 148 feet) legally would allow only one single family dwelling. Since the excess land provides utility equivalent to the standard site, it may sell at about the same price as the standard site. If so, the unit rates for this site are then $1,333.33 per front metre or $29.63 per square metre (approximately $406.78 per front foot and $2.75 per square foot). These resulting lower unit rates indicate that excess frontage and depth do not provide proportional utility.

Assemblage is a term often used interchangeably with plottage. However, in appraisal terminology it has a distinct meaning. Assemblage is simply the merging of adjacent properties into one common ownership or use. It may create plottage value, which is a value increment; or it may create excess land, which may result in a decreased unit value.

TOPOGRAPHY

The topography relates to the elevation and contour of the site. Analysis of topography is usually considered together with soils in order to relate drainage. A variance in topography and character may add to the value of a residential site by providing for a desirable form of architecture and pleasing amenity features. On the other hand, irregular topography may add to the cost of development for commercial and industrial uses.

CLIMATIC CONDITIONS

In some areas, climatic conditions may affect the value of lots that face in a certain direction. For example, prevailing winds may favourably or adversely affect lots according to their relation to the direction of the wind. Local shopping habits and pedestrian traffic patterns may affect the value of commercial sites for retail use. For example, if shoppers tend to favour the sunny side of the street, stores located on that side will probably do more business.

SERVICES AND UTILITIES

While considering the physical features of a site, the appraiser ascertains the availability of storm and sanitary sewers, water, gas, electricity and telephone.

ROAD AND STREET PATTERNS

Road and street patterns are influences to be considered in analysing neighbourhoods and also in appraising the individual site. Wide roads, limited access highways, one-way traffic street, median strips and boulevards, street lighting and sidewalks—any of these may be value influencing factors.

LANDSCAPING

Attractive landscaping of the site enhances its value. Trees, shrubs, lawns, flower beds and other improvements such as driveways, walkways and patios are improvements to the site and should be given consideration in the site analysis.

Locational Factors

Because of the immobility, the most significant single characteristic of any site is its fixed location. Location is always expressed in terms of the relationship of the site to surrounding and nearby facilities and nuisances.

LAND USE PATTERN

The location of various types of land uses within a city or neighbourhood are not determined at random but come about in response to the demand and requirement of these uses and are effectively controlled by the official plan of the area and by zoning by-laws and regulations.

ACCESS

Access is always estimated in terms of ease and convenience of getting to and from desired facilities like shopping, schools, churches, places of employment and recreation.

CORNER INFLUENCE

The effect of a corner location on value depends on the type of land use. Commercial corners provide the site with additional access and exposure for advertising purposes. Often, the side street provides added frontage for additional store fronts and entrances to upper apartments, leaving the main frontage free for display purposes.

Corners used for single family residential properties may have the reverse effect on value. Residential corners often provide no private rear yards, an amenity usually sought by a purchaser. Corner properties also cause the owner additional maintenance, usually by having to keep longer public sidewalks cleaned of snow in the wintertime. The above influences should be analyzed according to the local market and considered as a part of site valuation.

HAZARDS AND NUISANCES

The existence of nearby hazards and nuisances such as non-conforming land uses, noise, odour and traffic have a detrimental effect on residential property. The identification of elements of incompatibility or nonconformity provides one basis for the estimation of a possible loss in value due to locational obsolescence.

Legal-Governmental Factors

Legal factors deal with the lawful and restrictive uses of the site.

Legal Description. The legal description generally takes one of two forms: Lot and Plan Number where the site is located in a registered plan of subdivision; or by Metes and Bounds where the property is not located in a registered plan of subdivision but is rather a parcel of land carved out of a township lot in a concession.

Title Data. Essential facts include name of the registered owner of the property, legal description, mortgages registered against the property and any subsequent discharge of these mortgages, consideration paid for the property, liens, etc.

Zoning. Zoning is a political force affecting value. It is usually imposed by a municipality to allocate permitted uses in the economic sense and to provide a balance of uses within a prescribed area. The zoning by-law is the dominant legal force which sets out the minimum physical requirements of a site as well as the various uses allowed. Unless there is a reasonable probability that zoning could be changed, the site must be valued in accordance with its legal use.

Taxes and Assessment. Taxes and assessments normally are levied on an equitable basis. Occasionally a property is subjected to some form of special assessment which, in relation to other sites, reduces the net returns thereby affecting its value. This will be most important with sites used for income purposes and where a purchaser buys on the basis of net returns.

Easements. Deed restrictions such as easements reduce rights of ownership. The impact of easements on value may be minimal or extreme. For example, a pipeline easement may have little effect on farm productivity. On the other hand, a hydro easement covering a large part of a residential site may have severe restricting powers on the utility of the site.

Leases. Leases create split interests, dividing the value between the leaseholder and the freehold owner. A long term lease may preclude a fee owner from gaining maximum returns from a site for a specific future period. An example of this may be a lease over a total parcel of land which may be only partially improved. If, for example, the remaining land lease is for 25 years duration, the tenant could preclude the freehold owner from developing the excess land for 25 years. It may not pay the tenant to develop the land himself because he may not be able to recover the cost within that period. Consequently, the future use of the excess land may be postponed because of the lease.

Deed Restrictions. Private restrictions generally contained in the deed have varying effects on value. Subdividers often include restrictive covenants within a deed for the protection and interest of other owners within a preconceived plan. Oil companies often sell a former service station site and include a covenant that the site cannot be used to merchandise oil products during a specific future term.

Economic Factors

Most economic factors operate at the neighbourhood or market area level. Nevertheless, there are certain elements definitely related to site analysis which may be measured in terms of dollars.

Prices of Comparable Sites. These tend to set the range within which the value of the subject site is most likely to be found.

Tax Burden. The level of assessments, taxes and special assessments for utilities or streets is an important ingredient in the cost of owning the site or property. An important consideration is the comparative treatment of the subject site in relation to other competitive sites in the same area. The method of payment of taxes and special assessments can also constitute a burden on the land owner, and should be investigated.

Utility Costs. These are costs for utilities such as water and electricity. They should be considered in terms of both absolute and comparative levels.

Service Costs. These include such items as refuse collection, fire and police protection and the like. Both absolute levels and comparative treatment are important.

Inspection of Site

This phase of the inspection will include a detailed list of notes regarding the following site qualities:

1. Shape and boundaries of subject lot
2. Compliance with zoning regulations and by-laws
3. Grades and levels
4. Drainage pattern
5. Location of lot within the block
6. Quality of the soil
7. Views offered
8. Site improvements, description and measurements
9. Location of buildings on the lot
10. Land and building ratio
11. Orientation of buildings
12. Flood hazards, if any
13. Drives and approaches, ease of vehicular traffic
14. Public services
15. Dust, air pollution, odours
16. Landscaping
17. Aesthetic and architectural appearance of site and its improvements as a physical unit.

Improvements

From the appraiser's standpoint, improvements are usually distinguished as structures and site improvements. A careful and detailed description of all of the pertinent features of the improvements is necessary in every appraisal.

STRUCTURES

Structures are buildings erected on the land for a specific purpose, such as:

Single family dwellings

Figure 6
Site Data Form

1. LOCATION: _____
2. SHAPE OF LOT: _____
3. SIZE OF LOT: _____
   • WIDTH: _____
   • FRONTAGE: _____
   • DEPTH: _____
   • AREA: _____
4. UTILITIES:
   • ELECTRICITY ☐   • GAS ☐
   • WATER ☐   • TELEPHONE ☐
   • SEWERAGE ☐   • SIDEWALK ☐
   • STREET SURFACING ☐
5. TOPOGRAPHY:
   • LOT IN RELATION TO STREET GRADE: EVEN ☐ ABOVE ☐ BELOW ☐
   • LANDSCAPING ☐ TREES ☐
   • TOP SOIL ☐ THICKNESS: _____
   • SUBSOIL: GOOD DRAINAGE ☐ POOR DRAINAGE ☐
6. ZONING: _____
7. DEED RESTRICTIONS: YES ☐ NO ☐
   SPECIFY: _____
8. EASEMENTS AND ENCROACHMENTS: YES ☐ NO ☐
   SPECIFY: _____
9. TAX RATE: _____
   PROPERTY TAXES AS COMPARED TO THOSE IN COMPETING LOCALITIES:
   HIGH ☐ LOW ☐ SAME ☐
10. SPECIAL ASSESSMENTS: OUTSTANDING _____
                          EXPECTED _____

Multiple dwellings

Commercial use

Industrial use

Agricultural use

Special purpose:

(i)   Educational (schools, universities, etc.)

(ii) Institutional (hospitals, municipal, banks, etc.)

(iii) Others (recreational, entertainment, etc.)

SITE IMPROVEMENTS

These are other improvements usually *to* the site rather than *on* the site. Occasionally, some of these are included in the site analysis. Examples of site improvements are:

Fencing

Landscaping

Paved driveway

Swimming pool

Parking area

Outside lights, etc.

Inspection of Improvements

The importance of the physical on-site inspection of a subject property cannot be overemphasized. A well-planned, systematically-executed and thoroughly-recorded inspection of the property will provide the appraiser with the most important factual data required for his report. Although inspection and physical description of the property are essential to an appropriate appraisal, the emphasis is not placed entirely on physical characteristics. The functional utility of the improvements is equally as important.

SINGLE FAMILY DWELLING

The most common type of improvement the appraiser will be called upon to inspect is the family home. Depending on its design and the facilities offered by the structure, single dwellings could serve various purposes: temporary shelters, seasonal shelters (cottages) or residences (year-round homes). The inspection procedure for all these simple improvements is basically the same. The most important rule, as mentioned previously, is to conduct the inspection systematically, logically, and without omissions. Practising appraisers will have a check list in their repertoire to facilitate a fast and accurate gathering of the important information about dwellings. Most lending institutions will also provide their appointed appraisers with preprinted forms, requesting the data they require before issuing loans against the property.

The following information is usually required for providing an adequate description of the improvements in the appraisal report.

General Data

Type: function, architectural style, number of storeys

Size: building area, usable floor area

Age: chronological, effective by observed condition, remaining economic life expectancy

Construction Data

Foundation: type, material

Superstructure: type of structural skeleton, material, load-bearing members

Exterior walls: type, materials, finish, height

Interior partitions: materials, finish

Roof: structure, covering, flashing, soffits and gables

Closers: doors, windows, closing devices

Equipment Data

Heating: system, capacity, controls, units, fuel

Plumbing: fixtures, drains and vents, waste connections, means of waste disposal, storm sewer connections

Temperature control: air conditioning, humidity control, insulation, ventilation

Electricity: source of supply, materials, capacity, fixtures

Other: all items not covered elsewhere (T.V. aerial, telephone, intercom, vacuum system, etc.)

Functional Data

Layout: room arrangement, room size and shapes, ratio of size to use, circulation and traffic, ease of communication, stairways and corridors

Privacy: access to bedrooms, access to bathrooms, room orientation, views offered, soundproofing

Functional utility: floor, wall and ceiling finishes; heating adequacy, balance and economy; light; ceiling height; door and window operation; kitchen layout and cupboards; laundry facilities; bathroom layout; closet and storage facilities; door, window and cabinet hardware.

Garage or carport: type, size, capacity, doors, interior finish, accessibility

Extra features: list as encountered (fireplace, bar, recreation room, playroom, etc.).

It is beyond the scope of this text to discuss all items on this suggested check list in detail and offer the technical background information necessary to treat them expertly. There are excellent technical books available on construction, subject materials, structural design, home layout design, mechanical and electrical engineering, etc. One important thing to remember, however, is that the appraiser describing the property should avoid going into too much detail in unfamiliar areas. He should be absolutely confident before passing technical judgement regarding mechanical equipment, its adequacy, condition, or value and the same caution applies to structural considerations. One should also be careful to avoid the common error of the neophyte appraiser of using trade labels for material identification. The use of "Johns-Manville siding" instead of "asbestos siding," for example, should be avoided, because Johns-Manville produces a variety of materials and because several other companies also produce asbestos products. Similarly, "horizontal sliding sashless windows," should be used, not "Pierson windows" and "cement brick," not "Pilgrim brick," and so on. The appraiser should always identify components of the structure by their function and material, size or capacity, rather than by trade names when a great variety of similar products is sold on the market. Suppliers are in competition and their prices are usually comparable. The only exception to this rule occurs when certain products are known for their high quality and price well-above average. In this case, the items should be listed under "extra features" because they will affect improvement values. Products like "Andersen windows," "Crane plumbing fixtures," or "Sargent hardware" do enjoy an exclusive price status.

For the purpose of appraising single family dwellings, the inspection should be conducted with a standard newly constructed model home in mind. The appraiser should follow the method used by contractors in estimating construction costs. Any deviation from this model should be detected and recorded during the inspection as a price factor to be considered in the valuation. This base model usually has the following characteristics:

Clean, rectangular shape and "boxy" appearance with only four outside corners

Frame and brick veneer exterior

All rooms on one level only, or a clean full second floor

Concrete footings, concrete block foundations walls

Full unfinished basement

Concrete floor in basement and garage

1:4 pitch roof, asphalt shingles

Garage or carport under the same roof as the building

Two entrances only

Standard wood sash double-glazed windows, only 10% of floor area they serve

Interior drywall finish

Hardwood floors in living area, sheet vinyl in kitchen and bathroom

Minimum closet space required by the "Canadian Code of Residential Construction"

Hollow core slab doors throughout

1-4 piece bathroom

Cement laundry tub

Rental hot water tank

Forced air heating system

Exterior painting only, prime coat interior

100 amp. electrical service

Gravel driveway

Front yard sodded

The above list may require slight regional variations, but the average local unit price per square foot of building area will usually apply only to this model. Any deviation would, therefore, require an adjustment to the base price of the new construction.

INSPECTION OF MULTIPLE DWELLINGS

Multiple dwellings are residences erected to accommodate more than one family or tenant. The occupants either own, rent or share them. The most common types are:

Duplex or triplex units

Town houses

Condominiums

Co-operatives

Apartment buildings

The inspection procedure of multiple dwellings is similar in every respect to single units except that certain additional information is necessary, such as:

Quality of building from the point of view of easy maintenance

Number of units

Classification of units by size and number of rooms

Available storage space

Facilities (laundry, parking, amenities)

Rental information

Quality of tenants

Vacancy rates

Leasing arrangements

Quality of management

Operating and maintenance expenses

The main criteria for the appraiser is to inspect multiple dwellings with the eye of a well-informed, cautious investor. Factors having a direct bearing on the expected income and operating expenses should be given special attention.

INSPECTION OF COMMERCIAL, INDUSTRIAL AND SPECIAL PURPOSE PROPERTIES

This is a job for the skilled professional. The best advice is to call a qualified inspector to assist the client. The introductory section of this text emphasized that reading this text will not qualify the individual as an expert appraiser, and this warning is repeated here so that no misunderstandings will occur.

INSPECTION OF AGRICULTURAL PROPERTIES

The appraisal of an operating agricultural enterprise is a highly specialized field. A minimum requirement for an appraiser attempting it is a degree from an agricultural college. Farms in the urban shadow are inspected and appraised as a single family dwelling with a one acre lot around the principal residence, and the additional acreage is valued separately, with farm buildings treated as improvements. The appraiser must be aware of the possible extra value attributable to farm properties located on the fringe of urban development. Many of these properties have been subdivided and developed, which has increased their values tremendously. When giving listing advice the successful salesperson will keep these considerations uppermost in his mind.

Comparable Sales Data

Detailed data is also required on market sales of comparable properties. This information must be at least as detailed as the itemization of salient features of the subject property. It may serve as a basis for the application of certain valuation techniques, including:

estimating the value of the site by comparison;

estimating building construction cost by comparison;

estimating the value of the property by direct sales comparison;

deriving a monthly rental factor, gross rent multiplier or a capitalization rate.

The required information on the comparable sales includes:

date of transaction, to identify market conditions prevailing;

verified sales price

location, land use controls and environmental influences

physical characteristics and condition

functional utility

cost information

income and expense information

terms of financing

conditions of sale

Summary

This chapter emphasizes the importance of the study and analysis of trends that can affect property values, and introduces the use of graphs and other tools as a means of forecasting the effect of these trends.

Distinction is made between general and specific data and considerable detail is given as to the use of this data in the neighbourhood analysis, the site analysis and the analysis of the improvements.

The neighbourhood is defined and then analyzed in terms of both external and internal factors and forces that influence property values within its boundaries.

The site is analyzed on the basis of its highest and best use, with full consideration being given to the physical, locational, legal and economic factors that influence its value.

The inspection and analysis of the building and other improvements on the site involve not only the physical condition of the property, but also its functional utility.

Chapter 4

Step Four
Application of the Cost Approach

The cost approach is based on the Objective concept of value, which affirms that the "cost to create" is the main criterion in estimating value. The justification for using this approach in estimating the market value of a property lies in the principle of substitution, which maintains that no prudent purchaser will pay more for a property than the cost of producing or creating an equally desirable substitute property, provided that there is no delay in making the substitution. In other words, at any point in time, building values cannot rise above their reproduction cost.

The four basic steps in applying the cost approach in the appraisal process are:

1. Estimate the value of the site.

2. Estimate the cost of reproducing the existing improvements as though they were new on the effective date of appraisal.

3. Estimate the accrued depreciation suffered by the improvements from all causes.

4. Subtract the accrued depreciation from the reproduction cost new of the improvements and add the value of the site to arrive at an estimate of the market value of the property.

The diagram illustrated in Figure 7 may be helpful in understanding the overall theory of this approach to value.

Figure 7

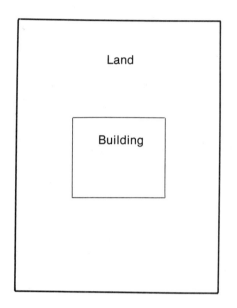

Step 1
Estimate Land Value $25,000

Step 2
Estimate Reproduction Cost of Building $40,000

Step 3
Estimate Accrued Depreciation $15,000

Step 4
Add the land value ($25,000) to the value of the depreciated building ($40,000 – $15,000 = $25,000) for an overall property value of $50,000.

Site Valuation and Methods

Although a separate site valuation is absolutely necessary in applying the cost approach to value, this is not the case with the application of the direct sales comparison approach or the income approach. However, it is often desirable and sometimes necessary to estimate a separate value of both the site and the improvements for other reasons such as:

1. To know the remainder value in the event the building is destroyed by fire

2. To determine the proper insurance coverage for the building(s) only

3. To establish the book value of the building as a basis for calculating allowable depreciation for tax purposes.

All sites, whether vacant or improved, must be valued as though they were vacant and available to be put to their highest and best use. There are four widely used methods of arriving at the value of a parcel of land:

1. The Comparative Sales Method

2. The Abstraction Method

3. The Land Development Method

4. The Land Residual Method.

The Comparative Sales Method

This method is based on a comparison of the property being appraised with the most recent sales data available on similar properties, preferably in the same neighbourhood. The assumption is made that if the subject property had been offered for sale, it would have been in competition with the comparable sales and, appealing to the same type of purchaser, would have been in the same market.

The steps to be followed in this method are:

1. Select a sufficient number of good comparable sites that recently sold in the area.

2. Gather all of the necessary data on these sales to be able to make a proper comparison.

3. Compare each of the comparable sales with the subject for differences that may exist.

4. Make the necessary adjustment to the sale price of each comparable for these differences.

5. Reconcile the adjusted sale prices of the comparables into an indication of the value of the subject.

All the comparable sales *must* be inspected at their location and all data recorded and verified as mentioned in the previous chapter on "Data Collection and Analysis." Since no two properties are identical, differences existing between each comparable sale and the subject property must be carefully noted. These may be differences in locational factors, in the frontage, depth, shape or size of the parcel concerned, the utilities available to it, conditions under which the sale was negotiated, the presence of easements or other restrictions, or changes in value due to the passage of time.

The comparable sales should now be analyzed to determine the degree of comparability with the subject property. If wide variances exist, the sale is probably not a valid comparable and should be discarded. Adjustments should be made to the remaining sales which have a high degree of comparability, to compensate for differences from subject. These adjustments are usually set out on a chart on which the differences from the subject property are shown and conditions surrounding the conclusion of the sale noted.

UNITS OF COMPARISON

For valuation purposes, sites are analyzed on the basis of units of comparison. The reduction of both the subject site and the comparable sites to a common unit provides a refined method of comparison in relation to the bulk price basis. The most common units of comparison are as follows:

Price per front metre. This unit is usually used to express values of residential lots, commercial lots, and sometimes industrial lots. It conveys no information about the depth or the width of the lot in question, but it is presupposed that the rate per front metre takes into consideration these other factors. Care must be taken in using this unit of comparison as recognition must be given to the fact that, beyond a useful width, the value of a site does not continue to increase proportionately with the additional frontage.

lake frontage

Price per square metre. The square metre unit of comparison is used in valuing apartment, commercial and industrial sites. It is valid when used on standard shapes of lots with usual depths for the neighbourhood. It can cause trouble when the lots have excessive depth and unusual shape.

Bulk basis. A price per lot basis is sometimes used when all the lots in the development area are approximately the same size and where a minor change in size may not affect the market value.

Price per suite. The unit of comparison for apartments is based on the price per suite. This takes into consideration the zoning of an area and the maximum permitted development of multi-family units under that zoning. It has meaning as a rule of thumb check but can cause trouble if used without determining the size of the apartment unit developed on the comparable sites.

Price per hectare. This is a unit of comparison used for agricultural land. It is also used as a unit of comparison for speculative type lands. Some rural appraisers may analyze and value land on the basis of price per section, price per half-section, or price per quarter-section.

THE ADJUSTMENT PROCESS

Having completed the work schedule concerning site sales and the analysis, the appraiser is ready to prepare the format for presentation of the sales and the adjustment chart for his report. The presentation of sales will include a short discussion relating the comparability of each sale to the subject property. Following this, the report will contain a summary chart of all sales and the various adjustments made to each. It should be remembered that any adjustments made to each sale should be rationalized either as part of each sale documentation or on a separate page. The actual adjustment process is the result of two basic factors, namely, what to adjust for and methods of making the adjustment.

WHAT TO ADJUST FOR

The main headings under which all adjustments are made are: Time, Location, and Physical Characteristics.

Time. The purpose of adjusting for this item is to allow for any price trend differential between the date of sale and the date of appraisal. Justification for this difference will be based on a price trend analysis of sales that took place at different times. For example, a particular type and size of site may have sold one year ago at $10,000 and again at $12,000 on or near the date of appraisal. The $2,000 price increase over that year reflects a 20% increase. To formulate a trend analysis chart, the appraiser will consider all sales and resales of sites over a period of the last year or two (and sometimes longer) from which he will make conclusions regarding the price increases over different periods of time. This provides a justification of adjustments when allowing for differences in time. The market, being imperfect, seldom provides conclusions as neat as the above. Consequently, the appraiser can only make judgements as best he can on the available sales and resales of similar sites or the same site. If the subject site is comparable in all respects to the sale described above, no other adjustment need be made. It follows, therefore, that the indicated value for subject site would be $12,000. In retrospect, what we have done is to adjust the comparable sale to the subject site allowing only for economic conditions prevailing at the two different dates.

Location. As discussed earlier in the section on Site Analysis, every site is subject to locational variations, all of which affect value. From the analysis of the subject site and each comparable, a judgement is made regarding the extent to which the locational forces affect the value of each. Such judgement on the part of the appraiser for locational differences must be impersonal and unbiased. If the analysis indicates that subject site is worth more than the comparable, such must be justified by relating these differences through comparable sales. Sales having equivalent locational factors to the subject may sell at $11,000 whereas sales in a less desirable location may sell at $10,000. Obviously, and for locational differences, people are prepared to pay $1,000 or 10% more for the subject property. In retrospect, we are saying that if the $10,000 comparable property were located as well as subject it would have sold for $11,000.

Physical. This is an all-embracing term which includes differences of frontage, depth, area, shape, topography and utility. To arrive at a more refined judgement reflecting these differences, it may be necessary to make separate judgements regarding each of the above physical differences, then combine the total adjustments to one fixed judgement difference. Market justification for physical differences can be found in sales of different groups of sites that reflect a difference. For example, 15 m sites may sell at $10,000 whereas 17 m sites may sell at $10,500 reflecting a $500 or 5% difference for the excess land. Similar comparisons can be made for variations in depth, shape and topography.

METHODS OF ADJUSTMENT

The two main methods of adjustment used by practising appraisers are the **plus and minus dollar adjustments** and the **plus and minus percentage adjustments**. Both, in reality, are the same. For clients lacking a mathematical flair, the dollar adjustment method may be easier to explain. As a general illustration of their similarity, assume that a comparable sold at $10,000; it required a plus $1,000 adjustment or 10% adjustment for location, and a minus $500 or 5% adjustment for physical characteristics. In tabular form, this would appear as follows:

Sale	Time	Location	Physical	Net Adj.	Ind. Value of Subject
$10,000	+ $1,000	+ $1,000	– $500	+ $1,500	$11,500
$10,000	+ 10%	+ 10%	– 5%	+ 15%	$11,500

It is important to reiterate that the various adjustments are summed and applied to the sale price of the comparable which produces an indication of value for the subject site. Plus signs indicate that the comparable property is inferior to the subject. Minus signs indicate that the comparable property is superior to the subject.

From the above table it can be seen that the net adjustment is a culmination of the three adjustments and is applied directly to the sale price. **Actually, it is proper to adjust for time first and then total the other factors and apply that sum to the sale price after the adjustment for time.** The reason for this is to bring all sales to the same economic base and then adjust for other differences. This method will provide a slight mathematical variance in the indicated value of the subject site when using the percentage method.

Example

Sale Adjusted For Time	Location	Physical	Net Adj.	Indicated Value for Subject
$11,000	+ $1,000	– $500	+ $500	$11,500
$11,000	+ 10%	– 5%	+ 5%	$11,550

Note: Using the percentage adjustment method the indicated value for subject is $50.00 higher ($11,000 x 1.05). Since all adjustments are based on the appraiser's best judgement, the slight variance between the methods is unimportant, when the individual adjustments are themselves relatively small.

Figure 8 illustrates the adjustment process in tabular form. It is recommended that a tabular analysis chart similar to this be included in the appraisal report when this method is being used to estimate the value of the site.

The Comparative Sales Method is the most commonly used and the most easily understood method of valuing land. Its validity depends on the careful selection of comparable sites and the application of proper adjustments for differences which have been revealed during the investigation.

Abstraction = Subtraction

The Abstraction Method *— subtraction*

The Abstraction Method is simply a process of starting with the known sale price of a property and then estimating the value of the building, which is then subtracted from the property sale price, leaving the residual amount as the value of the land.

Generally speaking, this method is a poor indicator of value and is used only as a rough rule. The appraiser must be able to justify the value of the building and be sure there are no unusual motivations for the sale or excess profit taking. It is seldom used as a single tool to indicate the value of a site.

The Land Development Method *— Hypothetical Subdivision*

This is a method of valuing land which is ripe for development for urban use.

A hypothetical plan of sub-division is projected on the site. The gross

Figure 8

Tabular Analysis of Comparative Sales

Sale No.	Front Metre	Sale Price	Price Per f.m.	Time Adj.	Time Adj. $/m	Phy.	Other Adjustments Loc.	Total	Adjusted Price/f.m.
1	18	$30,000	$1,666.67	+ 5%	1,750.00	− 8%	+ 20%	= + 12%	$1,960.00
2	15	28,000	1,866.67	—	1,866.67	+10%	− 5%	= + 5%	1,960.00
3	15	27,000	1,800.00	+10%	1,980.00	+ 5%	− 5%	= 0	1,980.00
4	17	29,000	1,705.88	+ 5%	1,791.18	—	+ 7%	= + 7%	1,917.00
5	15	29,500	1,966.67	—	1,966.67	− 5%	+ 5%	= 0	1,967.00
6	18	33,720	1,873.33	—	1,873.33	−10%	+15%	= + 5%	1,967.00

ORIGINAL DATA   *TIME*   *ADJUSTMENTS*   *UNITS*

Assuming that the subject site had a frontage of 15 metres, the value range indicated by the Direct Sales Comparison Method would be $28,755 to $29,700. After reconciliation, the appraiser may place the greatest weight on the value per front metre indicated by the most comparable—say Sale #5.

In that event, the Market Value of the subject property would be estimated at $1,967.00 per front metre, or $29,505—rounded to $29,500.

(Adjustments could have been made in dollar amounts rather than percentages, and cents could have been rounded to the nearest dollar).

sales of the lots is estimated and from this total income, costs of development, including the profit of the developer, are deducted. The balance remaining will be the value of the land. In using this method, it is necessary to also take into account the effect of a time lag in marketing the lots and the resultant costs of carrying the property. The final estimate will represent the price which a developer would pay for the land in the light of its total potential for development.

Since this method involves many assumptions and cost estimates which are difficult to substantiate, it is time consuming and costly, and has limited use.

The Land Residual Method — *income approach*

This method of site valuation is based on the principle of surplus productivity, which affirms that the net income remaining after satisfying the requirements of labour, co-ordinating services and capital is attributed to land and sets its value through the capitalization process.

At this point in the study of real estate appraising, the method of handling income valuations has not yet been discussed, so it is only possible to touch on the method briefly. This method will be more thoroughly treated in the "income approach to value" section of this text.

The Land Residual Technique is used to find a value estimate of a site which is readily adaptable for use as the location for an income producing property. A hypothetical building which will develop the site to its highest and best use is projected on the site and the cost to erect it is calculated based on current building cost.

The potential annual gross income is estimated based on current rental rates. From this, an allowance for vacancy and bad debts is subtracted to arrive at the effective gross income. The expenses to operate the building are then deducted resulting in a net income attributable to the property. This net income figure already has had the cost for labour and co-ordination taken into consideration because they were part of the operating expenses of the building. To satisfy requirements of capital, an amount equal to the building value, times the combination of the interest rate plus the recapture rate, is deducted from this net income and the resulting net income is attributable to the land value as detailed in the principle of surplus productivity.

The value of the site is found by Capitalizing this net income attributable to the land by a rate which represents the current return required by investors in the market place for this type of investment.

Estimate of Reproduction Cost New

The second step in the cost approach is to estimate the cost of reproduc- *(exact home)* ing the improvements as though they were brand new on the effective date of the appraisal. If there is more than one building on the site then a separate reproduction cost new should be estimated for each building. Furthermore, a separate reproduction cost new should be estimated for those site improvements which were not included in the site valuation.

As mentioned earlier, inherent in this cost approach is the principle of substitution. The principle implies that cost sets the upper limit of value and cost and value are equal:

principle of sub. (same size ~ utility)

exact duplicate

Cost sets the upper limit of value. It is the reproduction cost new *identical utility* and not the replacement cost that generally sets the upper limit of *current cost.* value. Estimating the reproduction cost new is the starting point in arriving at the contribution that the building, in its present condition, makes to the value of the total property (site and building).

Although this reproduction cost new is the cost to create a replica or duplicate of the building being appraised on the date of appraisal, it is the *cost to the purchaser* that must be estimated, not cost to a builder or contractor. Thus, "cost" includes the builder's overhead and profit, *and* all indirect costs. Also note that this reproduction cost new is the cost to produce the subject building as though it was *new* as of the valuation date; it is not historical cost.

Cost and value are equal. This could be true, but it is not usually the case. By definition, cost is the price paid to create a commodity; i.e., it is the *production cost*—an objective concept of value. *Value*, however, is defined as the present worth of future benefits—a subjective concept of value. Ideally, cost and value are equal when:

(1) The improvements are brand new.

(2) The improvements represent the highest and best use of the site.

(3) The improvements are not affected by functional or locational obsolescence.

(4) The expected return from the improvements justifies their cost.

Quite often cost can be higher than the value: for example, where

Cost higher than value.

there is a super-adequacy built into the improvements (a 508 mm. wall is built when only a 254 mm. wall is required). Here, the cost minus depreciation (even though new) equals the value of the building.

Reproduction versus Replacement Cost

It is reproduction cost rather than replacement cost that is the subject matter of the estimate. Reproduction cost is the cost of exactly reproducing, as of the date of appraisal, the actual building that is to be appraised using identical materials at current costs. Many older buildings would not be replaced today with the original materials, style and layout. It is recognized that in certain respects older buildings are obsolete. Nevertheless, whatever obsolescence is inherent in these structures, it is in fact depreciation and should and will be accounted for as depreciation in the next step in the cost approach.

In contrast to *reproduction cost* we often hear the term *replacement cost*. This is the cost of replacing the subject building with a new structure of the same *size* and *utility* using current technology, materials and equipment instead of trying to reproduce it detail by detail. Appraisers most often use reproduction cost in the cost approach rather than replacement cost. In the first place, by so doing, the appraiser is preparing an estimate of the cost of the actual building on the site whereas a replacement cost estimate is nothing more than the appraiser's opinion of the type and style of building that would replace the utility of the old building. In fact, the replacement building may be even more valuable than the old building because of its newness, reduction in maintenance and operating costs. Therefore, replacement cost is not an exact measure of obsolescence as some persons think. However, if replacement cost were used properly, all items of functional obsolescence would be eliminated.

Methods of Estimating Reproduction Cost

The appraiser has several alternative methods of estimating reproduction cost new. The choice is usually governed by the significance of the cost approach in arriving at the final estimate of value; the degree of accuracy required; the qualification of the appraiser in applying the more sophisticated methods of costing; and the method to be used in calculating the accrued depreciation. However, the appraiser should realize that no matter which method is selected, building cost estimates can rarely be exact. Even though the cost of building materials and labour can usually be determined for any date, the cost necessary for a contractor to combine them into a building cannot be estimated with the same accuracy. The profit required by contractors varies depending on the present availability of work. It is not uncommon for bids on the same building tender to vary by substantial amounts. Four methods of estimating reproduction cost are:

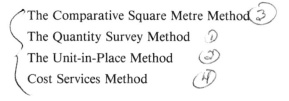

The Comparative Square Metre Method ③

The Quantity Survey Method ①

The Unit-in-Place Method ②

Cost Services Method ④

THE COMPARATIVE SQUARE METRE METHOD

The Square Metre Method simply involves the ascertainment of the known current average cost per square metre of construction of similar buildings, and the multiplication of this unit cost by the number of square metres in the structure whose cost is to be estimated. The accuracy of this method of cost estimating depends on the refinements made by the appraiser to cover the differences that exist between the properties from which the unit cost is derived and the property being appraised. It would be quite incorrect to ascertain the square metre cost of a two storey house and apply this unit cost as a basis in estimating the cost of a one storey house. It would also be incorrect to apply the square metre cost of an oddly shaped one storey house to estimate the cost of a more conventionally shaped one storey house. Herein lies the possibility of inaccuracy in this method and the appraiser should be sure that the properties from which a cost estimate is derived are truly comparable to the property being appraised. Secondly, the appraiser should be certain that his cost estimates are current and apply as of the effective date of the appraisal.

Figure 9 illustrates in tabular form the comparison process of estimating reproduction cost by this method.

Best & most detailed

THE QUANTITY SURVEY METHOD — *looks @ detailed construction*

The quantity survey method is the process used by building cost estimators and contractors. It involves the preparation of an inventory of the quantity of each material, and the time (hence cost) of its placement in the structure, with additional allowances for contractor's overhead, risk and profit.

This method of costing is the most accurate and reliable method and yet it must be remembered that it is only an estimate. It gives sufficient

Figure 9

Tabular Analysis—Comparative Square Metre Cost

Sale No.	Sale price of property	Land Value	Building Cost	Adjustments in $	Adjusted Bldg. Cost	Area m²	Fully Adjusted Bldg. Cost Per m²
1	$61,200	$20,000	$41,200	− 2,000	$39,200	130 m²	$301.54
2	65,000	21,500	43,500	+ 1,000	44,500	147 m²	302.72
3	63,000	19,000	44,000	− 2,150	41,850	140 m²	298.93

39,200 ÷ 130

Area of subject building = 140 m²

Indicated reproduction cost new of subject building

140m² at $300 per m² = $42,000

detail for purposes of measurement of physical deterioration. Its disadvantages are that it is time-consuming and costly. However, it is a very useful tool in the hands of an experienced appraiser. It is highly unlikely that the real estate practitioner would ever resort to this technique.

[Variation of Quantity Survey Method.]

THE UNIT-IN-PLACE METHOD *— components of construction in phases.*

The Unit-in-Place Method is sometimes referred to as a modified quantity survey. It involves the pricing of the various units (by area or volume in the structure), such as walls, openings (doors and windows), partitions, floors, rooms, and so forth. By way of illustration the average cost of a wall may be a certain number of dollars and cents per square metre of wall surface (the rate applied to one side only). This cost is for all of the wall, such as the studs, interior lath, plastering, painting, and exterior siding—painted—all completed and in place. Or the Unit-in-Place Method may be used in greater detail to estimate the cost-in-place of such items as concrete foundation walls, cement block walls, footings, exterior brickwork, rough framing, roofing, plastering, wiring, etc.

This method has the advantage that it is much faster than the quantity survey once the appraiser knows the unit prices. The disadvantages are that it is still time-consuming and costly.

COST SERVICES METHOD *— most used: standardized, good reputation*

Three of the building cost services presently available in Canada are: Lansdowne's Construction Cost Handbook, Boeckh Building Valuation Manual, and Marshall and Stevens Valuation Quarterly. All cost services work on the same basis by providing unit cost information for a bench-mark structure. They represent average generalized data for particular types of construction. The adjustments made by the appraiser are for specific structural variations, time, and geographic location. The cost service provides the figures for making individual physical adjustments, for example, for hot water heat instead of forced hot air as was costed in the bench-mark structure, or for wooden windows instead of aluminum windows, or for many other variations. These adjustment figures may be given as lump sum adjustments, or a square foot or cubic foot rating.

The cost services supply index figures which are used as multipliers to update the cost estimate for individual geographical areas based on material and labour cost changes and the passage of time.

Most cost services publish their data in manual form with periodic supplements which provide multipliers for geographic differences and a time adjustment related to the base rate contained in the original benchmark cost.

The Cost Services Method can be a fast method of estimating building costs. Care should be taken, however, to assure that the appraiser has made appropriate adjustments to the base building specified in the cost services, as it compares to the subject building. It can be said that no two buildings are identical and for this reason adjustments will always have to be made. The accuracy of the cost service will depend on the appraiser's accuracy in making these adjustments.

Figure 10 illustrates the use of the Base Square Foot method in estimating the reproduction cost new for a two storey residence as of valuation day—December 31, 1971.

Estimate of Accrued Depreciation

/PAST

The third step in the cost approach involves the estimation of accrued depreciation. This is an essential step in the cost approach because without a complete analysis of loss in value from all causes, the cost approach may not lead to a meaningful value conclusion.

The Nature of Depreciation

Depreciation is often defined as a loss in utility and hence value from any cause. In appraisal theory only the improvements are subject to depreciation. Land is considered a non-wasting asset and although land value may decrease (or increase) because of market forces, this is not depreciation. There are two distinct types of depreciation with which the appraiser will be concerned: Accrued Depreciation, used in the cost approach; and Accruals for Depreciation, applied in the income approach.

ACCRUED DEPRECIATION

This is sometimes referred to as "Diminished Utility" and is the difference between the reproduction cost new and the value of the improvements as of the date of the appraisal. It is *accrued* because the depreciating factors have been at work from the time the building was constructed to the date of the appraisal.

ACCRUALS FOR DEPRECIATION

/FUTURE

This is the basis of provision for the recapture or recovery of capital invested in the improvement over its remaining economic life. It is some-

Figure 10

The following describes the **Base Square Foot Method** for a 2 story residence with a built-in garage. It shows the procedure required to determine a Valuation Day Value using the Boeckh System.

1. **Building Description** (known data)
   Detached single family house
   2 story with full basement and built-in garage
   Aluminum siding
   Dimensions 31'6" x 32'0" ground floor
   Location — Ottawa
   Age — 10 years (effective)

2. **Living Area, Ground Floor Area, Boeckh Ratio**
   Ground floor area 31'6" x 32'0" = 1008 sq.ft.
   Upper floor area   31'6" x 32'0" = 1008 sq.ft.
   Total living area   2016 sq.ft.

$$\text{Boeckh Ratio} = \frac{\text{Ground Floor Area}}{\text{Ground Floor Perimeter}} = \frac{1008}{(31'6'' + 32'0'') \times 2} = \frac{7.94}{\text{rounded to 8.0}}$$

3. **Base Building Cost** (Base Square Foot Method)
   Select from the 2 story model, Boeckh Ratio of 8
   Exterior walls of aluminum siding
   Base Square Foot Cost $13.94
   Base Building Cost =
   $13.94 x 2016 sq.ft. **$28,103**

4. **Modified Base Building Cost**
   Basement deduction is unnecessary as
   subject building has basement
   similar to model . . . .   —

5. **Other Additions**
   Built-in garage . . . . (deduct)   **−672**

6. **Total Building Cost**
   Sum of 3, 4 and 5 . . . .   **$27,431**

7. **Local Reproduction Cost New**
   Ottawa location modifier .93
   Local Reproduction Cost New =
   .93 x 27,431 . . . .   **$25,511**

8. **Depreciation Allowance**
   10-year-old building with normal
   depreciation of 14% . . . . . . (deduct)   **−3,572**

9. **Building Value December 31, 1971** . .   **$21,939**
                    (rounded to $21,940)

times referred to as "Future Depreciation." This form of depreciation is used in the income approach to value and has no place in the cost approach.

Causes of Accrued Depreciation

Accrued depreciation is brought about by physical, functional and economic causes known as physical deterioration; functional obsolescence and locational obsolescence.

(1) PHYSICAL DETERIORATION

This is an impairment of the physical condition of the improvement due to wear and tear, decay and structural defects. The rapidity of physical deterioration will depend largely upon the quality of the original structure, workmanship and materials, the use or abuse of the property, and the general maintenance of the structure during its life. Deterioration can generally be seen and easily recognized.

(2) FUNCTIONAL OBSOLESCENCE *(OVER IMPROVED — SUPER ADEQUACY)*

This is a loss in utility, hence in value, due to the inability of any component part of the structure or any item of equipment to perform its proper function in terms of today's standards and requirements. It is inherent in the property and is a loss from reproduction cost new as at the date of appraisal caused by deficiency, inadequacy, superadequacy, unattractive or unacceptable style, poor or inefficient design; lack of modernization, etc. Functional obsolescence is more likely to emerge with the passage of time, however, a component part of the structure or an item of equipment can be outmoded or unacceptable in terms of today's standards even in a brand new building.

(3) LOCATIONAL OBSOLESCENCE

This is a loss of value to the property (affects both land and building) brought about by some external factor. In the past this type of obsolescence was referred to as "Economic Obsolescence" and although the term is still widely used it is somewhat of a misnomer in that all elements of accrued depreciation are "economic" in their impact on utility and value. Locational Obsolescence is a term more descriptive of the cause of *this* type of depreciation.

The effects of this locational obsolescence must be strong enough to be properly measured in the market place. It is not sufficient to believe that the inharmonious locational factors should cause a loss in value in the subject property; it is necessary that the appraiser have evidence that it *does* cause a loss in value.

Examples of locational factors which can cause a loss in value to a residential structure could be all-night drive-in restaurants, service stations, truck routes adjacent to the property, inadequate land use controls and protection, changes in zoning, etc.

Understanding of Specific Terminology

Before proceeding with the estimation of accrued depreciation it is important to have a clear understanding of certain terminology to be used in this section on measuring accrued depreciation.

ECONOMIC LIFE - *utility of life*

This is the period of time over which a new structure may reasonably be expected to be competitive in the market in the use for which it was designed. It is the period of time over which the structure may profitably be utilized. It is said that the structure reaches the end of its economic life when it becomes a burden to the land. Economic life is the base from which total utility is estimated.

REMAINING ECONOMIC LIFE

This is the period of time from the date of appraisal to the expiration of the economic life of the structure. It is the length of time that the prudent investor will leave his money invested in the property. The remaining economic life is the base from which remaining utility is estimated.

EFFECTIVE AGE - *actual age minus improvements*

This is the age of the structure based on the use and care it has received. It is also the difference between Economic Life and Remaining Economic Life of the structure. Effective age may be greater or less than actual or chronological age depending on maintenance, condition, etc.

ACTUAL OR CHRONOLOGICAL AGE

This is the actual number of years that have passed since the structure was built. The following "Life Line" diagram below will be helpful in visualizing these concepts.

```
                        35 years
    ◄─────────────────────────────────────────────►
                      Economic Life
    1962
            15 years                    20 years
    ◄──────────────────►◄──────────────────────────►
          Effective Age        Remaining Economic Life
            20 years
    ◄──────────────────────────►
          Actual Age
```

This diagram illustrates the various "Life concepts" of a house built in 1962. It is actually 20 years old as at 1982. Because it has received above average care and maintenance its effective age is judged to be only 15 years. The combination of the Effective age and the Remaining Economic Life represent the Economic Life of the property.

CURABLE AND INCURABLE ITEMS

Component parts of the building are classified into curable or incurable items, simply to measure the loss in value suffered by that item.

Curable Items: Those items that the typical purchaser would repair or replace immediately on taking possession; where the cost of repair or replacement is offset by the increased utility; and where it is economically sound to repair or replace.

Incurable Items: Items which are not new or modern; which have suffered some loss in value but which the typical purchaser would not consider repairing or replacing immediately; and where the cost of effecting a cure is greater than the anticipated increase in utility; i.e., not economically sound to cure.

INCURABLE PHYSICAL DETERIORATION

Incurable physical deterioration is broken down into short-lived and long-lived items, simply to measure the loss in value in this category.

Short-lived items are those component parts of the structure whose life expectancy is less than the remaining economic life of the structure as a whole.

Long-lived items are those components which are expected to have a life expectancy equal to the remaining economic life of the structure as a whole and which the typical purchaser would not cure, not because it is not technically or physically possible to cure, but because it would not be economically sound to do so.

Methods of Estimating Accrued Depreciation

The three most common methods of measuring depreciation, are the Age-Life Method, the Modified Age Life Method, and the Observed Condition (Breakdown) Method.

AGE-LIFE METHOD

This is the easiest technique and was the first method used to measure accrued depreciation. Because of its many weaknesses, it is used mainly as a rule-of-thumb check for one of the other methods.

In the age-life method an estimate is made of both the effective age of the building and its remaining economic life. The effective age and remaining economic life together comprise the economic life of the building. The ratio of the effective age to the economic life times the reproduction cost new of the structure is a measure of the accrued depreciation. Effective age may, or may not, represent actual or chronological age, as maintenance, design and location are factors which may increase or decrease the aging process. The remaining economic life of the building will, in most instances, represent something less than the remaining physical life.

Example

Assume that a building has an actual age of 15 years, an estimated effective age of 10 years and a remaining economic life of 40 years. Its reproduction cost new on the date of appraisal is $71,750. The accrued depreciation estimated by the age-life method would be as follows:

Actual age	15 years
Effective age	10 years
Remaining economic life	40 years
Reproduction cost new	$71,750

$$\frac{10 \text{ (the effective age)}}{50 \text{ (the economic life)}} = 20\%$$

Accrued depreciation $= 20\% \times \$71,750 = \$14,350$.

Many practising fee appraisers use variations of this method where the property being appraised does not suffer any loss in value due to functional or locational causes.

It should be noted here that the age-life method only accounts and measures physical deterioration.

THE MODIFIED AGE-LIFE METHOD

As the name implies, this is a modification of the age-life method in that it breaks down the component parts of the structure into two categories and measures physical deterioration for each category separately. The categories are Curable Physical Deterioration and Incurable Physical Deterioration.

Curable Physical Deterioration. This includes items which a prudent buyer would anticipate correcting before or shortly after taking possession. It is termed "curable" because it would be economically sound to correct this physical deterioration and the buyer would be justified in so doing. Curable items can usually be classed as deferred maintenance. Examples of this condition are repair or replacement of floor coverings or roof; repairs to broken windows, doors or downspouts; or repainting or wallpapering. The cost to cure is the measure of the loss in value or depreciation.

Incurable Physical Deterioration. This applies to items which are not yet ready to be cured and which it is not economically sound to cure at the time, since the cost of correcting the condition or effecting a cure will be greater than the anticipated increase in value. It should be noted that correction of the condition may well be physically or technically possible, however, the criterion is whether it is economically sound to cure. All component parts of the structure not accounted for, or measured for depreciation under the first category of curable physical deterioration must therefore be measured under this second category. For the purpose of measuring the loss of value, these remaining component parts of the structure are classified as either short-lived or long-lived.

The **short-lived** items are those components that are not yet ready to be replaced but that will require replacement sometime before the end of the remaining economic life of the structure. In other words, their life expectancy is less than the remaining economic life of the building. Here the depreciation is measured by taking the ratio of the effective age (by observation) of the component to its life expectancy, expressed as a percentage and applied to the reproduction cost new of the item.

(Actual age in lieu of effective age could be used for certain components whose actual ages are readily ascertainable.)

The **long-lived** components are those items which will have suffered some physical deterioration but will not require replacement at any time during the economic life of the structure. Here the depreciation is measured by taking the ratio of the effective age of the structure as a whole to its economic life, expressing it as a percentage, and applying it to the *balance* of the reproduction cost new (i.e. the total reproduction cost new less the reproduction cost of the items considered under physical deterioration curable and the incurable short-lived).

Taking the same example used to illustrate the estimate of depreciation by the age-life method, but breaking it down further as required for the estimate by the modified age-life method, the calculation would appear as follows.

Figure 11
Accrued Depreciation Schedule

I	Estimated Value of Site						$17,000
II	Estimated Reproduction Cost New					$71,750	
III	Estimated Accrued Depreciation						

1. Curable Physical Deterioration

	R.C.N.	C. TO C.	
a) Painting Interior	1,600	1,700	
b) Eaves and downspouts	500	650	
c) Doors	400	450	
	2,500	2,800	$ 2,800

2. Incurable Physical Deterioration

a) Short-Lived

Component	Rep. Cost New	Eff. Age	Life Exp.	Dep. %	Dep. $	
Heating	1,400	15	20	75	1,050	
Kitchen Built-In	1,500	15	20	75	1,125	
Tiled Floors	400	9	12	75	300	
Hardwood Floors	800	15	20	75	600	
Exterior Painting	1,000	1	4	25	250	
Roof Covering	1,000	15	20	75	750	
Electric Fixture	600	15	20	75	450	
Hot Water Heater	350	15	20	75	263	
	7,050				4,788	4,788

b) Long-Lived

Reproduction Cost New		71,750
Less Reproduction Cost New from—		
(i) Physical Curable	2,500	
(ii) Physical Incurable		
short-lived	7,050	9,550
Total long-lived		62,200
Effective Age 10 years, R.E.L. 40 years 10/50 x 62,200 =		12,440
Total Physical Deterioration		20,028 $20,028

Again, it should be noted that although this is an excellent method of measuring physical deterioration, it does not consider any loss in value that may result from functional or locational obsolescence. For this reason, appraisers will use this method only when it is apparent that the property being appraised is not affected by any functional or locational obsolescence, or they will use it as part of another method which does account for loss in value due to functional and locational obsolescence.

THE OBSERVED CONDITION (BREAKDOWN) METHOD

This method of estimating accrued depreciation is considered to be the most provable method since it breaks down the structure into its component parts and measures all physical, functional and locational causes of depreciation based on an observation of the actual physical and functional condition of the structure. Under this method, accrued depreciation is broken down and measured under the following classifications:

1. Curable Physical Deterioration
2. Incurable Physical Deterioration
   Short-lived
   Long-lived
3. Curable Functional Obsolescence
4. Incurable Functional Obsolescence
5. Locational Obsolescence

For an example of the measure of accrued depreciation under each of these categories, refer to the illustration of the accrued depreciation schedule in Figure 11.

1. Curable Physical Deterioration. Measured by the Cost to Cure.

2. Incurable Physical Deterioration.

Short-lived. Measured by taking the ratio of the effective age (by observation) of the component to its life expectancy, expressed as a percentage and applied to the reproduction cost new of the item. (Actual age in lieu of effective age could be used for certain components whose actual ages are readily ascertainable.)

Long-lived. Measured by taking the ratio of the effective age of the structure as a whole to its economic life, expressing it as a percentage and applying it to the *balance* of the reproduction cost new (i.e. the total reproduction cost new less the reproduction cost of the items considered under physical deterioration curable and the incurable short-lived).

3. Curable Functional Obsolescence. Measured by the Cost to Cure. Cost of the new item installed less the depreciated cost of the obsolete item (the depreciated cost of the obsolete item is its reproduction cost new less the physical deterioration already deducted).

4. Incurable Functional Obsolescence. Measured by taking the estimated or actual rental loss arising from the deficiency and multiplying it by the monthly rental factor if it is a residential property, or by the gross rent multiplier if it is an income property. (The Monthly Rental Factor, M.R.F., is the relationship between the monthly rent and the sale price. The Gross Rent Multiplier is the relationship between the annual gross rent and the sale price.

5. Locational Obsolescence. Measured by multiplying the rent loss resulting from this locational obsolescence by the Monthly Rental Factor (M.R.F.) if a residential property and by the Gross Rent Multiplier (G.R.M.) if an income property. The resultant figure will be the value loss to both land and building. Since the locational obsolescence of the site is already reflected in its estimated market value, only the value loss to the improvement(s) must now be charged as depreciation.

Again, taking the same example as used previously in calculating the accrued depreciation by the age-life and modified age-life methods, but adding items of functional and locational obsolescence, the extended and full accrued depreciation schedule will appear as illustrated in Figure 11.

Figure 11
Accrued Depreciation Schedule

RCN OF BLDG. $71,750   LADD $17,000

I   Estimated Value of Site
II   Estimated Reproduction Cost New
III   Estimated Accrued Depreciation

1. Curable Physical Deterioration—IMMEDIATE

	R.C.N.	C. TO C.
	—DEFERRED MTN.—	
a) Painting Interior	1,600	1,700
b) Eaves and downspouts	500	650
c) Doors	400	450
	2,500	2,800 $ 2,800

2. Incurable Physical Deterioration (COMPONENTS) OR AGE/LIFE(Ratio)

a) Short-Lived (COMPONENTS)

Component	Rep. Cost New	Eff. Age	Life Exp.	Dep. %	Dep. $
Heating	1,400	15	20	75	1,050
Kitchen Built-In	1,500	15	20	75	1,125
Tiled Floors	400	9	12	75	300
Hardwood Floors	800	15	20	75	600
Exterior Painting	1,000	1	4	25	250
Roof Covering	1,000	15	20	75	750
Electric Fixtures	600	15	20	75	450
Hot Water Heater	350	15	20	75	263
	7,050				4,788 4,788

b) Long-Lived —STRUCTURE

Reproduction Cost New   71,750
Less Reproduction Cost New from—

(i) Physical Curable   2,500
(ii) Physical Incurable
short-lived   7,050   9,550
Total long-lived   62,200

Effective Age 10 years, R.E.L. 40 years   10/50 x 62,200 =   12,440

Total Physical Deterioration   20,028 $20,028

3. Curable Functional Obsolescence – NOT IN TODAYS STANDARDS

   Modernization of cupboards   2,000

   Less depreciated costs of

   existing cupboards   −685   1,315

4. Incurable Functional Obsolescence

   a) Deficiency

      Monthly Rent Loss x M.R.F.

      $10 x 180   1,800   1,800

   Total Functional Obsolescence   3,115   3,115

5. Locational Obsolescence

   Monthly Rent Loss x M.R.F.

   $5 x 180 = 900   [SECONDARY SITE 1/4 H]

   Ratio of Land to Building 1:3

   75% of 900   675

       675

   Total Locational Obsolescence   675

   Total Depreciation (all causes)   23,818   23,818

IV   Depreciated Cost of Building   47,932

   plus depreciated cost of outside improvements   1,800

   Total Depreciated Cost of all Improvements   49,732   49,732

   Market Value by Cost Approach $66,732

Rounded to $67,000

MRF = MO. RENTAL / SF.
    SF / MO RENTAL

Final Step in the Cost Approach

The final step in the cost approach is simply a mathematical calculation. It involves calculating the value of the building, which may be simply expressed as an equation:

Reproduction Cost New – Accrued Depreciation = Value of Building

The value of the site and the value of other outside improvements (if any) are added to the value of the building to arrive at the value of the property.

Summary of the Cost Approach

Estimated value of site		$17,000
Estimated Reproduction Cost New	$71,750	
Estimated Accrued Depreciation	23,818	
Depreciated Cost (or value) of Building	47,932	
Depreciated Cost (or value) of other improvements	1,800	49,732
Market Value by Cost Approach		$66,732

ACCRUALS - FUTURE

accrued Dep - "Diminished utility" a is the diff-bet.
repod cost new & the value of the improvements
as of the date of appraisal.

Chapter 5

Step Five
Future Income

Application of the Income Approach

Introduction

The income approach to value is based on the theory that the value of a property is the present worth of the future income which this property is capable of producing. It involves the capitalization of the net income, by an appropriate rate, into an indication of value. The value of all types of income producing properties is related to some degree to the income producing potential of these properties—the higher the potential income, the higher will be the price that the property will command on the market. **Factors other than income which must also be considered are:**

The type of building

The age of the building

The location

The neighbourhood

Competing neighbourhoods

Condition of the improvements

Type of business to be conducted in the premises

The quality of the tenant

All these factors have a direct bearing on the value of an investment type property, but all these factors being equal, then the higher the potential income the higher the value.

what is the present worth of a future Benefit?
(Principle of Anticipation)
Market Value - Prin. of Substitution

Steps in the Income Approach

The application of the income approach to the valuation of investment type properties can be broken down into five important steps.

1. Estimate the potential annual gross income less likely vacancies and bad debts.
2. Estimate the total annual operating expenses.
3. Calculate the net operating income.
4. Select the appropriate capitalization rate.
5. Using the appropriate method of capitalization, discount the net income into value.

First Step—Estimate the Potential Annual Gross Income, Less Likely Vacancies and Bad Debts.

This involves the estimation of the annual or twelve-month rental income that the subject property is capable of producing. This rental income must be the amount which the property is capable of producing when developed to its Highest and Best Use.

The most exact method of estimating gross income is to make a comparison in the market with properties similar to the one being appraised, and which are currently being rented to their best advantage. The projected income would be based on market rent rather than actual or contract rent.

The appraiser may start his analysis of the income potential of a property by reference to the owner's income statement. Such a statement is a very useful guide, but it is not necessarily a reliable one for appraisal purposes. It frequently happens that an owner's statement shows income that is not entirely applicable to the current year, or that is representative only of an abnormal vacancy condition in existence in that particular year. It may be that some of the rental units were being modernized, rehabilitated or renovated and their potential is not represented on the statement.

The main point is not to accept the owner's statement as representative of typical management conditions without first checking the figures against averages or the experience of comparable properties. All valuations for listing purposes should be made on the basis of typical management for the type of property being appraised. The statement the appraiser finally uses to support the income figure should be his own reconstructed statement representative of typical, prudent management or ownership of the property.

It sometimes happens that a property, at the time of appraisal, is not developing the highest income which it is capable of producing.

If such is the case, the first job of the appraiser is to determine the rental income that would exist if the property was rehabilitated, remodelled, or modernized to produce this highest income. It must also be recognized that this income is produced only after the expenditure of money on the contemplated program of rehabilitation, modernization or remodelling. Therefore, it becomes necessary to subtract from the final estimate of value obtained by the income approach, the cost of such a program together with a profit to the owner for risking the expenditure of money to develop the property to its Highest and Best Use. The appraiser is valuing the property as it exists before the changes have actually been made, but the income on which the estimate of value is based is only capable of being earned after the building has been renovated, etc.

Mention has been made of the terms rehabilitation, modernization and remodelling. These terms are often used as if they were the same, and in consequence, reference is made to remodelling when rehabilitation is contemplated. It is important for the appraiser to remember that these are three distinct functions, as is seen from the following definitions:

Rehabilitation is restoration to good condition without changing plan, form or style.

Remodelling is changing the plan, form or style to correct functional or economic deficiencies.

Modernization is the replacement, in modern style, of outmoded aspects of the structure and equipment.

Basing the gross income on any such projected program should only be done after a careful study of the economic feasibility of the program in light of the principle of contribution, principle of increasing and decreasing returns, principle of highest and best use and the principle of balance. To be economically sound, the cost of making the changes has to be less than the resulting increase in value.

When projecting income on this basis, the cost of the program of remodelling, etc., must be deducted from the capitalized value of the projected income.

Next, estimate the probable vacancy or credit loss that the subject property may be expected to suffer based on the same conditions used in calculating the potential gross income, that is, market rent, typical management and the most profitable use of the property.

It is important to recognize that location, age and style of properties, and the types of tenants which can be attracted, all affect the income and vacancy rate. Even a prime grade property, under a long term lease, may not be rented 100% of the time when considering the entire remaining economic life.

When the amount allowed for vacancies and bad debts is subtracted from the total estimated gross income, the result is known as the Effective Gross Income. This amount is the closest the appraiser can come to what may be called the actual gross income that the property is capable of producing.

Second Step—Estimate the Total Annual Operating Expenses

Net income is the most important factor in arriving at an estimate of value. Before net income can be established, it is necessary to project typical operating costs in the form of an operating statement. This operating statement is simply a record of all the annual expenses chargeable to the operation of the real estate being appraised. These expenses are the ones necessary to maintain the level of effective gross income and operate the building for its remaining economic life.

As with gross income, operating costs can be obtained from the actual operation of the property being appraised. These should only be a guide to assist the appraiser, however, in his own projection of typical management conditions.

The history of the operation of the building being appraised may not reflect competent management. It may not cover all the items of expense that should be properly included. It may not show all the operating costs necessary to maintain the gross income flow. It is necessary, therefore, to refer to the operations of similar properties when reconstructing the operating expense statement to ensure that expenses are in line with those suffered by similar properties.

One other source of comparative expense data is in the form of published studies of a variety of properties. These studies equate the expenses to a cost per unit or show them expressed as a percentage of the Gross Income. For example, the publication might state that apartment buildings up to 24 units have expense ratios of 42-44% of the Gross Income. This is very good reference material as it will alert the appraiser to drastic variations between the subject and other similar properties. The expense per unit would be stated at "so much" per apartment and this could be applied to the subject as a cross check. Remember, it is only typical, ongoing expenses which are necessary to generate the Gross Income that you must be concerned with. It is also worth reiterating that it is only the *annual* expenses that should appear in your reconstructed expense statement. We are not concerned with monthly expenses, however if they are quoted on that basis they must be converted to a yearly base. This of course also applies to all other aspects of an operating statement, through from the Gross Income to the Net Operating Income.

Operating Statement Expenses

At this stage, a hard look at all expenses which are likely to appear in an operating statement is in order.

Taxes. The annual realty taxes are calculated by multiplying the total assessed value of the property, land and buildings, by the current mill rate. It must be noted that income tax and business tax of the owner should not be included in the operating statement.

Insurance. This is an essential operating cost and should be considered under the headings of fire, liability, boiler, plate glass, theft, etc. The proper premium for only those classes of insurance that relate to the functioning of the particular property should be included and only on the basis of a one-year premium.

Management. This is a necessary item of expense. All properties require good, competent management to function properly and this charge must be made whether the owner is the manager or this function is performed by a management company. The fee is usually calculated as a percentage of the effective gross income.

Utilities. These usually include heating, electricity, gas and water if they are paid by the owner.

Cleaning and Caretaking. This usually includes the cleaning of common areas, window cleaning, snow removal, gardening, etc. If the custodian is doing this work and gets a free suite in return, the income that the suite could otherwise produce would be included in the gross income estimate and the total custodial cost charged in the expense statement.

Wages. Costs of wages can include those for custodian, superintendent, gardeners and others as required for the proper functioning of the property. Included under this heading are the costs of owner's contributions to Unemployment Insurance, Canada Pension Fund and Insurance plans.

Supplies. This is the annual amount necessary for the purchase of paper supplies, light bulbs or tubes and miscellaneous cleaning items as required for a typical operation.

Miscellaneous. Operating statements for valuation purposes usually lump a few items of expense together including legal fees, auditing costs, advertising and sundry purchases. Quite often these expenses are calculated on the basis of a percentage of the effective gross income with the rate being dependent on the type of property being appraised.

Other major areas of expense that must be carefully considered include roof repairs, window caulking, tuck pointing, exterior painting, and structural repairs and may include repair of heating, lighting and plumbing equipment depending upon lease provisions.

Decorating costs may include interior maintenance and minor repairs. Necessary provision for this category of expense varies according to local custom and may also vary from year to year depending upon supply and demand factors for this type of space.

Alterations are another phase of maintenance. If sufficiently extensive, they may be charged to capital addition instead of to annual expenses. The lessor may perform some alterations in the space rented, the expense of which may not be amortized by additional rental, or which alternately, may be paid for by the tenant.

Although these expenses tend to vary at least in part according to occupancy, they also tend to be concentrated in some years. They therefore must be stabilized to an average annual figure. For some types of buildings, especially apartments, office buildings, and hotels-motels, published figures are available indicating the average annual and national maintenance costs per square metre of building area. Maintenance and repair activity must be compatible with typically competent management.

EXCLUDED ITEMS

In reconstructing the operating expense statement for appraisal purposes, certain operating expenses appearing in the owner's statement must be omitted. This is necessary since the owner's statement is usually prepared not for appraisal purposes but for income tax reporting. Such items would include:

Business Tax. This tax is levied on the business being conducted on the property and should be accounted for only when appraising the business and not when appraising the real property, which is the case here.

Depreciation or Capital Cost Allowance is an allowable expense for income tax purposes and will invariably appear in the owner's expense statement. This item is omitted in the appraiser's reconstructed statement but provision is made in the capitalization rate to recapture the capital invested. To include it the expense statement as well would amount to double recovery.

Interest on Mortgage or Loan. This is not a direct cost of calculating net operating income. Though interest charges may be tax deductible, they benefit the owner and not the property.

Capital Improvements (Capital Outlays). These are expenditures that enhance the value of the property and are designed to increase its income producing potential. As such, they are not operating expenses necessary to maintain the potential gross income. Quite often the owner of an investment property has to make supplementary capital expenditures. These are for the replacement of short life component parts of the structure, for mechanical equipment, and for alterations, renovations and chattels. Unless these cash outlays can legitimately be accounted for as expenses for repairs or maintenance, the full amount of these capital cost expenditures must be added to the remaining capital cost of the structure, and not included as an operating expense. It should be carefully noted, however, that where the overall rate used in capitalizing the net income has been derived from an analysis of comparable properties, whose operating expenses included reserves, then reserves must either be included in the reconstructed operating statement or the overall rate recalculated after adding back the reserves to the net operating income of the comparable properties.

Reconstructed Operating Statement

Once the component items that should be included in the typical operating expense statement for the type of property have been identified and stabilized on an annual basis by the appraiser, he can reconstruct the operating statement using the stabilized figures for the appropriate items.

Figure 12 is an apartment property owner's three year income and expense statement. Figure 13 is the appraiser's reconstructed statement. A comparison of these two statements will indicate the nature of the reconstruction required for appraisal purposes.

ANCILLARY MEANS EXTRA INCOME.

Figure 12

Owners' 3-Year Operating Statement

	3 yrs ago	2 yrs ago	1 yr ago	Ref. No.
REVENUE				
Rent Collections	$372,761	$379,964	$385,630	
Parking and laundry receipts	33,975	35,375	35,450	
	406,736	415,339	421,080	04
EXPENSES				
Realty taxes	50,940	52,375	53,642	05
Superintendent—salary	9,500	10,500	11,500	06
Janitor—salary	4,800	5,280	5,808	07
Water	8,450	8,720	8,950	08
Electricity	974	1,135	1,217	09
Fuel	3,700	5,150	7,200	10
Insurance	6,000	—	—	11
Maintenance and repairs	5,800	6,800	4,000	12
Painting and decorating	16,400	10,500	18,400	13
Supplies	850	1,020	1,224	14
Legal and audit	1,000	1,650	1,250	15
Elevator maintenance	1,200	1,200	1,200	16
Depreciation	42,000	57,000	54,150	17
Mortgage payments	206,750	206,750	206,750	18
	358,364	368,080	375,291	
Net Income	$ 48,372	$ 47,259	$ 45,789	

Figure 13

Appraiser's Reconstructed Statement

POTENTIAL GROSS INCOME

Rent Collections
18 1-bedroom units x $300 per month x 12 =	$ 64,800	
78 2-bedroom units x $375 per month x 12 =	351,000	
	415,800	01

Ancillary Income
Parking—96 spaces x $20 x 12 = 23,040		
Laundry—96 x $10 x 12 = 11,520	34,560	02
Total gross income potential	450,360	
Less allowance for vacancy and bad debts–5%	22,518	03
Effective gross income	$427,842	04

OPERATING EXPENSES

Realty taxes ASSESS x MILL RATE	$ 54,100	05
Superintendent	17,000	06
Janitor	9,989	07
Water	9,216	08
Electricity	1,320	09
Fuel	9,000	10
Insurance	2,700	11
Maintenance and repairs	4,000	12
Painting and decorating	18,000	13
Supplies	1,469	14
Legal and audit	1,300	15
Elevator maintenance	1,500	16
Management—3%	12,835	19
Total operating expenses	142,429	

NET ANNUAL OPERATING INCOME $285,413

The following is a detailed explanation of how the appraiser arrived at the reconstructed operating statement.

1. The **potential annual gross income** from rental collections is based on the market rent for each apartment with all suites fully rented. This amount would include the rental income which would be collected for the suites presently occupied, rent free, by the superintendent and the custodian.

2. In addition to normal rent, each tenant must pay $20 per month for **parking** and $10 per month for **laundry** facilities.

3. A **vacancy allowance** of 5% of both rental and ancillary income is based on current competitive conditions as indicated by a survey of comparable properties in the area.

4. The **previous year's gross income** represented actual cash collections. The effective gross income represents the total potential gross income less an allowance for vacancy and bad debts.

5. The **current year's taxes** as shown in the reconstructed operating statement were derived by multiplying the present assessment by this year's mill rate.

6. The **superintendent's salary** was adjusted upwards from last year's, at the same rate of increase as previous years. Added to it is the allowance of the free 2-bedroom suite.

7. The **custodian's salary** was adjusted upwards from last year's, and at the same rate as previous years. The allowance of a free 1-bedroom suite occupied by the custodian was also added to his salary.

8. **Water costs** based on present consumption worked out to an average of $8 per suite per month. This checked out very closely to published figures for water consumption costs in this general area.

9. **Electricity expenses** pertain only to the public areas and to the equipment. The average current cost is estimated at $110 per month. Tenants are responsible for their own consumption, individually metered to each suite.

10. **Fuel costs** have been rising rapidly over the last three years. The estimate for the current year is based on the average consumption for the last three years at a rate quoted by the gas company for this year's heating season.

11. The three year **insurance premium** for fire and extended coverage, and for public liability, has increased from $6,000 to $8,100. One-third of this has been charged to the current year's operating expense.

12. As a result of the property rehabilitation program undertaken almost two years ago, it is expected that **expenses** for **maintenance and repairs** will remain the same as last year's expense, for at least the next two or three years.

13. The current years **painting** and **decorating expense** is based on the cost of $500 per suite once every three years, and a total cost of $10,000 to paint the public areas and exterior trim, once every five years.

14. **Expenses** for **supplies** have been increasing steadily by 20% per year. The current year's expenses are projected on this basis.

15. **Legal and audit expenses** for the current year are an average of the last three years.

16. **Elevator maintenance expenses** are based on a new three year contract of $1,500 per year.

17. **Depreciation** is not a deductible expense for the purpose of deriving net operating income for appraisal purposes.

18. **Mortgage payments** of principal and/or interest are not a deductible expense in arriving at net operating income.

19. **No management costs** were reported in the owner's statements. Typical management cost for this type of property and operation in this area is 3% of the effective gross income.

Note: Earlier, it was mentioned that reserves for replacements of short life components, equipment and chattels should **not** be included as an operating expense. **The cost of replacing worn out items is a capital cost expenditure which must be capitalized.** The only time the appraiser may be justified in including a reserve for replacement of such short life components in the operating expense statement is when the market indicates that this is normal practice adopted by property owners in the area; and when the overall rate used by the appraiser in capitalizing the resulting net income has been extracted from comparable properties treated in the same way, i.e. provision was also made for "reserves for replacement" in arriving at their net operating income.

Third Step—Calculate the Net Operating Income

This is the net operating income earned by both land and building before depreciation and is often found abbreviated in various appraisal texts as N.I.B.D (Net Income Before Depreciation) or simply N.O.I. (Net Operating Income). It is arrived at by deducting the operating expense estimate from the effective gross income.

Fourth Step—Select the Appropriate Capitalization Rate

Capitalization in the appraisal process is the discounting of future receivables (the net operating income) by a capitalization rate.

An investor in real estate is entitled to a return *on* the money invested in the property (in both land and building) and is also entitled to a return *of* the monies invested in the building. This latter return is known as recapture. The reason that the investor is only entitled to the recapture **of** the monies in the **building**, is because the building is a wasting asset and it will be worthless when it reaches the end of its economic life. On the other hand, the investor is not entitled to the recapture **of** monies invested in the **land**. This is because land is considered to be a non-wasting asset and it is presumed that the investor will recover the monies invested in the land when it is sold.

The rate of return *on* the invested capital is generally referred to as the "Discount" rate. The rate of return *of* the invested capital in the building is called the recapture rate. The capitalization rate applied to the net operating income generated by the property is known as an overall rate. It blends the discount rate and the recapture rate in the same proportion as the ratio that the land value bears to the building value. (See example on facing page.)

In actual practice the appraiser usually acquires the overall rate directly from the market by dividing the net income of comparable properties by the sale price of these same comparables. A tabular analysis of three comparable properties designed to illustrate the derivation of the overall rate appears on the facing page.

It should be noted here that the overall rate was developed from properties that had sold for all cash. This same procedure can be adopted for properties that are financed, provided of course, that the financing of each of the comparable is the same as the subject property which is producing the income to be capitalized.

Example

Assume that an investor purchases a small investment property for $150,000 cash. The allocation to land is $30,000 (or 20% of the investment) and $120,000 (or 80% of the investment) to the building. Assume also that the rate of return on the total investment (discount rate) is 10% and that the building is judged to have a remaining economic life of 40 years.

The annual "return of" or recapture rate is simply calculated by dividing the remaining economic life (R.E.L.) into 100%. The 100% represents the return of all of the investment in the building. The calculation would therefore be 100 divided by 40 = 2.5%.

The blended "Overall Rate" can be calculated by adding the weighted average of the discount rate applicable to the land value to the weighted average of the discount rate and recapture rate applicable to the building.

e.g. 20% land value at 10% or .20 × .10 = .02

plus 80% building value at 12½% or .80 × .125 = .10

Overall Rate 12% or .12

Tabular Analysis
Derivation of the Overall Rate

Sale No.	Cash Sale Price	Net Income Before Depreciation	Price Earning Ratio or Overall Rate
1	$136,900	$16,500	.1205 or 12%
2	166,500	20,000	.1201 or 12%
3	154,000	18,500	.1201 or 12%

Indicated overall rate applicable to subject is 12%

Fifth Step—Using the Appropriate Method of Capitalization Discount the Net Income into Value

Having arrived at the net income earned by the property, and having selected the appropriate capitalization rate, the next and final step is to capitalize or discount this income into an indication of the value of the property.

Methods of Capitalization

There are various methods of capitalization including:

1. The Direct Method
2. The Mortgage-Equity Cash Flow Method
3. The Annuity Method
4. The Mortgage Coefficient Method
5. The Discounted Cash Flow Method

Only the first two methods mentioned above will be covered in this chapter. The Annuity Method, the Mortgage Coefficient Method, and the Discounted Cash Flow Method, all require a comprehensive understanding of the arithmetic of money at compound interest and the use of compound interest and discount factor tables which are beyond the scope of this text.

The Direct Method of Capitalization

This method of capitalization is applied to income produced by an investment property which is not under lease or where the lease period is a short term one and the income does not have the characteristics of a long term annuity.

The capitalization is a simple mathematical process using the following formula.

$$I/R = V$$

WHERE: I is the Net Operating Income.

R is the Capitalization Rate.

V is the Value.

Residual Techniques

This direct capitalization process involves the use of three different techniques depending upon the source of the income. These techniques are:

Property Residual Technique

Building Residual Technique

Land Residual Technique

PROPERTY RESIDUAL TECHNIQUE

Capitalization of net income earned by the property (both land and building) into an indication of the value of the property. Here a blended rate known as the overall rate is used to capitalize the income. This blended rate includes the interest on the money invested in both land and building plus the recapture of only the investment in the building itself.

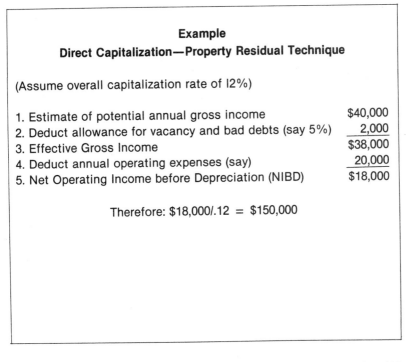

Example
Direct Capitalization—Property Residual Technique

(Assume overall capitalization rate of 12%)

1. Estimate of potential annual gross income	$40,000
2. Deduct allowance for vacancy and bad debts (say 5%)	2,000
3. Effective Gross Income	$38,000
4. Deduct annual operating expenses (say)	20,000
5. Net Operating Income before Depreciation (NIBD)	$18,000

Therefore: $18,000/.12 = $150,000

DISCOUNT **Example** (LEFTOVERS)
Direct ~~Capitalization~~—Building Residual Technique

(Assume land value at $30,000; a ~~capitalization~~ discount rate at 10%; remaining economic life of building 40 years.)

1. Estimate of Potential Annual Gross Income	$40,000
2. Deduct allowance for vacancy and bad debts (say 5%)	2,000
3. Effective Gross Income	$38,000
4. Deduct annual operating expenses (say)	20,000
5. Net Operating Income before Depreciation (NIBD)	$18,000
6. Deduct income earned by land $30,000 at 10%	3,000
7. Residual Net Income to Building	$15,000

Value of Building   I/R = V

$$15,000/.125 = \$120,000$$

Plus Value of Land $30,000

Value of Property $150,000

BUILDING RESIDUAL TECHNIQUE

Capitalization of net income earned by building into an indication of the value of the building. Here the capitalization rate is a composite rate including the interest rate plus the full recapture rate. To be able to calculate the net income attributable to the building the value of the land must be a known factor.

```
                          Example
          Direct Capitalization—Land Residual Technique

  (Assume building value of $120,000, a capitalization rate of 10%;
  remaining economic life of building 40 years.)

  1. Estimate of potential annual gross income              $40,000
  2. Deduct allowance for vacancy and bad debts (say 5%)     2,000
  3. Effective Gross Income                                 $38,000
  4. Deduct Annual Operating Expenses (say)                  20,000
  5. Net Operating Income before Depreciation (NIBD)        $18,000
  6. Deduct income earned by building $120,000 at 12 1/2%    15,000
  7. Residual Net Income to Land                            $ 3,000


     Value of Land             I/R = V
                        3,000/.10 = $30,000

     Plus Value of Building        $120,000

     Value of Property             $150,000
```

(handwritten annotations: "Discount" above "Direct", "discount" above "capitalization")

LAND RESIDUAL TECHNIQUE

Capitalization of net income earned by land into an indication of the
value of the land. Here only the interest rate is used as the capitalization
rate. To be able to calculate the net income attributable to the land, the
value of the building must be known.

(handwritten: ckk – discount – recapture – overall)

The Mortgage Equity Cash Flow Method

This cash flow method of capitalization is probably the most common and most valid method of investment analysis and appraisal, particularly for small income producing properties which are bought and sold on the basis of their annual cash flow.

Today virtually all investment real estate is financed with one type of mortgage or another. Where this is the case, the value of the property, at any point in time, is a *function* of the amount of cash equity which must be invested over and above the amount of debt.

This cash flow method involves the Annual Dividend Rate, which is the annual rate of return on the original equity invested. It is found by dividing the annual cash flow by the original equity:

$$C.F./E = y$$

WHERE: CF is the Cash Flow (Cash Flow is derived by subtracting the annual debt service from the net operating income.)

E is the original equity invested

y is the annual dividend rate

THE CASH FLOW METHOD IN REAL ESTATE INVESTMENT ANALYSIS

Example

A property is being offered for sale at $400,000 subject to a new first mortgage of $300,000 to be fully amortized over a period of 25 years at a S.A.R. of 9.75%. Monthly principal and interest payments are $2,633.10. The average annual net operating income is forecasted to be $37,000 per annum. Equity capital is normally attracted to this type of investment for dividend rates ranging from 5 to 6%. The problem is to analyse this investment in the light of the given data.

Analysis:

Average Annual Net Operating Income	$37,000
Less Debt Service $2,633.10 x 12	31,597
CASH FLOW:	$ 5,403

INDICATED DIVIDEND RATE:

$$\frac{CASH\ FLOW}{ORIGINAL\ EQUITY} \quad \frac{5,403}{100,000} \quad .05403 = 5.4\%$$

In view of the fact that equity capital is normally attracted to this type of investment at dividend rates ranging from 5 to 6%, it must be concluded that the asking price at $400,000 is a realistic one.

THE CASH FLOW METHOD IN REAL ESTATE INVESTMENT VALUATION

The value of a partially financed property is a function of the amount of cash equity which must be invested over and above the mortgage debt. Therefore, if the appraiser can ascertain the amount of the mortgage at the time of the appraisal, then all that need be estimated is the value of the equity. This can be done by the Equity Residual Technique.

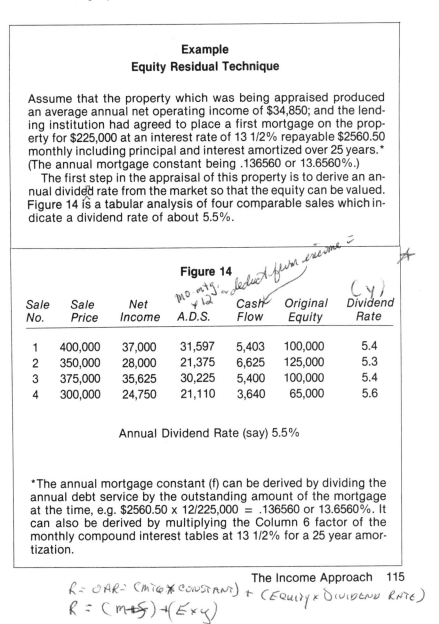

Example
Equity Residual Technique

Assume that the property which was being appraised produced an average annual net operating income of $34,850; and the lending institution had agreed to place a first mortgage on the property for $225,000 at an interest rate of 13 1/2% repayable $2560.50 monthly including principal and interest amortized over 25 years.*
(The annual mortgage constant being .136560 or 13.6560%.)

The first step in the appraisal of this property is to derive an annual dividend rate from the market so that the equity can be valued. Figure 14 is a tabular analysis of four comparable sales which indicate a dividend rate of about 5.5%.

Figure 14

mo. mtg. × deduct from income

Sale No.	Sale Price	Net Income	A.D.S.	Cash Flow	Original Equity	Dividend Rate (y)
1	400,000	37,000	31,597	5,403	100,000	5.4
2	350,000	28,000	21,375	6,625	125,000	5.3
3	375,000	35,625	30,225	5,400	100,000	5.4
4	300,000	24,750	21,110	3,640	65,000	5.6

Annual Dividend Rate (say) 5.5%

*The annual mortgage constant (f) can be derived by dividing the annual debt service by the outstanding amount of the mortgage at the time, e.g. $2560.50 x 12/225,000 = .136560 or 13.6560%. It can also be derived by multiplying the Column 6 factor of the monthly compound interest tables at 13 1/2% for a 25 year amortization.

$R = OAR = (mtg \times constant) + (Equity \times Dividend Rate)$

$R = (m \times f) + (E \times y)$

Valuation:

Average annual N.O.I.	$34,850
Less annual debt service	30,726
Cash Flow	$ 4,124

Equity Contribution CF/y = 4,124/.055 = $ 74,982
Mortgage Contribution   =   225,000
Indicated Value   = $299,982

Rounded to $300,000

Normally the lending institution would say that they would lend (say) 75% of the appraised value rather than quote an amount. In this case the appraiser would not know either the amount of the mortgage or the amount of the equity. Therefore, to estimate the value of the property he would have to develop an overall rate, then use the basic capitalization formula of:

$$I/R = V$$

The Cash Flow formula for deriving an overall rate is

$$(M \times f) + (E \times y)$$

M = Ratio of mortgage to value
f = annual mortgage constant
E = Ratio of equity to value
y = Annual Dividend Rate

Taking the same problem as before, the value of the property is arrived at as follows:

Valuation:

Average Annual N.O.I.	$34,850

R   = (M x f) + (E x y)
     = (.75 x .136560) + (.25 x .055)
     = .102420 + .013750
     = .116170
I/R = V   34,850/.116170 = $299,991

Rounded to $300,000

Summary

The income approach to value rationally assumes that there is a relationship between the net income a property is capable of earning and its value at any given moment in time.

The appraiser starts by estimating the potential annual gross income for the current year and subtracts from this a market-derived vacancy and credit loss allowance for the year to arrive at the effective gross income. Operating expenses are then deducted from the effective gross income, leaving net income.

The final step in this approach requires the selection and application of a proper rate in discounting the net income into value by a mathematical process known as Capitalization.

Chapter 6

Step Six
Application of the Direct Sales
Comparison Approach

Introduction

If you have completed a "Market Analysis" for the purpose of estimating a probable selling price you have already experienced the subtle character of the Direct Sales Comparison Approach. This technique is a simple but effective value measurement tool, one which is easily understood by the courts and the average person on the street. It is particularly appropriate in the valuation of single family residential properties although it is also employed in the appraisal of complex income producing properties.

You may have experienced this valuation technique, not only in the merchandising of real estate, but also in your every day life style as a consumer of retail items, since it is *basically a technique of comparison*. No doubt the last time you purchased a car or a basket of groceries you compared prices prior to the purchase. The same basic concept applies in the comparison of properties which recently sold to the one which you are attempting to value for listing purposes. However, a word of caution is appropriate at this time. As the technique appears simple and logical, it can also be easily underrated or misunderstood. The market is a complex, sometimes unpredictable creature and it is only when you fully appreciate these qualities that you are prepared to interpret its likely value signals.

This Direct Sales Comparison Approach, sometimes called the "Comparative" or "Market Data Approach," is a valuation method whereby the property being appraised is compared with similar properties that have been sold, offered for sale, rented, or offered for rent. Since no two properties are identical, adjustments must be made for any differences between the comparables and the subject property. When reconciling to arrive at a preliminary value conclusion, the greatest weight is given to actual sales of truly comparable properties made at or nearest the effective date of appraisal to reflect comparable economic conditions. Inherent in this concept is the underlying Principle of Substitution, which affirms that where a property is replaceable, its value tends to be set by the cost of acquiring an equally desirable property, provided that there is no delay in making the acquisition.

This value measurement tool is very effective when a sufficient number of sales of similar properties have taken place. The sales must be closely scrutinized in order to isolate areas of differences which will require adjustments. These adjustments will eliminate the differences and the result is a probable value estimate for the subject property.

Rationale of the Direct Sales Comparison Approach

The price for which a property is most likely to sell depends on general factors such as national, regional and neighbourhood data as well as specific factors such as the comparable sales data.

Market value is the type most commonly estimated and its definition indicates those factors to be considered when making a judgement as to the price for which a property is most likely to sell. Whatever the sale price of a property, it is certainly based on the market data of competitive property sales. The concept of market value embodies such factors as:

allowing a reasonable time to find a purchaser

both buyer and seller being informed as to all uses

neither buyer nor seller being under pressure to buy or sell

As previously discussed, this approach is most effective when there are sufficient quantities of accurate, reliable market data which are properly analyzed. These data must be evaluated, as though through the eyes of a typical purchaser, without the intrusion of the appraiser's personal viewpoint. The best data are from the neighbourhood in which the subject property is located and current to the date of appraisal.

Thus, the substance of the Direct Sales Comparison Approach is to search out the recently sold competitive properties and through an adjustment process, develop an indication of what they would have sold for if they possessed the physical and economic characteristics of the property being appraised. Such value indications are developed for several comparable sales and should, when rounded, cluster around one figure, thus providing a value indication for the subject property.

Steps in the Direct Sales Comparison Approach

1. Gather all comparable sales, listings and rentals.
2. Locate and check pertinent information on each.
3. Analyze the data regarding differences both in time of sale and other factors.
4. Compare each sale to subject property making the necessary adjustments.
5. Reconcile the data and make a final value estimate.

Sources of Data

Registry and Land Titles Offices

Appraisers own files

Real estate offices

Assessment records

Zoning records and maps

Private sources

Multiple Listing Service

Teela Sales Service

Newspapers

Personal tours of the neighbourhood

Principals and participants in sales

Data Requirements

The Direct Sales Comparison Approach involves locating a number of comparable properties that have recently sold in the local market. These sales are then adjusted to provide an indication of value for the subject property. To make effective comparisons, detailed information must be acquired for each sale. The data gathering program must be systematic so that all pertinent and salient characteristics are itemized for both the subject and comparable properties. By so doing, meaningful comparisons can be made.

When locating and checking the sales, it is usual to find that many are not comparable and should be discarded immediately. The basic test is whether the comparable selected is competitive with the subject property in the mind of a typical purchaser.

Salient Information Required For Both Subject and Comparable

Legal:

instrument number

date of sale

date of registration

grantor (vendor)

grantee (purchaser)

legal description

sale price and financing

chattels included

previous sales

verification with one or both principals

zoning

assessment

Physical:

lot size, characteristics, landscaping and topography

architectural style

building size (sq. ft. or cubic foot)

number of rooms

number of baths

room layout

age and construction

special features such as fireplace, built-ins, recreation room, storms and screens, etc.

accessory buildings, such as garage, etc.

notes regarding physical and functional obsolescence

notes regarding neighbourhood influences

notes regarding desirability

The subject property will be described in detail in the early part of the appraisal report. The comparables are presented in systematic form with only the pertinent elements of comparability, so that the reader of the report can visualize these elements of comparability. Sales should be verified to assure a bonafide arms length market transaction.

Quality and Quantity of Data

QUALITY OF DATA

To provide an accurate value estimate, sales should be:

within the local market

at or near the date of appraisal

truly comparable sales

bonafide arms length transactions

QUANTITY OF DATA

The availability of market data varies both for the different types of real estate and the velocity of sales during any given period of time. Thus, there is no set number of sales that should be presented. Under slow market conditions, sales will be few. In an active market, sales will be plentiful. For residential property it is suggested that from four to eight truly comparable sales will provide the basis for an accurate value estimate of a subject property.

Units of Comparison

The purpose of using units of comparison is to bring the comparable property sales more in line with the subject property. Although it may be possible to compare one whole property with another whole property, a more refined comparison can be made if each is reduced to some common denominator such as sale price per square foot or unit. Differences should be relatively small, however, otherwise the property compared may be in a different market. An example of this may be the attempt to adjust for differences in comparing a 2,000 square foot residence with an 800 square foot residence.

$$\frac{SP}{EGI} = GRM$$

effective
gross
income

M & F – high

GRM – low

The units of comparison used should reflect the thinking of a typical buyer. For example, the sale price per square metre of a factory building, the sale price per suite or per room for an apartment building, the Gross Rent Multiplier for most income producing properties.

The Gross Rent Multiplier is the ratio of the effective gross annual rent to the sale price of the property. Since no adjustments are made in using this unit of comparison, care must be taken to assure a high degree of comparability between the comparable properties from which the G.R.M. is extracted and the subject property, to whose effective gross income the G.R.M. is subsequently applied. An example of establishing the G.R.M. from one comparable property is as follows: Assume that a commercial property sold for $350,000 and produced an effective gross income of $63,636 at the time of sale. G.R.M. = 350,000 divided by 63,636 = 5.5.

Elements of Comparison

Elements of comparison refer to the various component parts of a sale which may require adjustment due to differences between it and the subject property.

Sometimes in new developments, property sales identical to the subject may be found and need little or no adjustments. Normally, however, the salesperson will not be so fortunate and will have to make item by item comparisons.

Having established that the sales to be used are truly comparable, and within the competitive market segment of the subject property, adjustments for variables fall under four main headings: Time, Location, Physical Characteristics and Motivation.

TIME

The Principle of Change states that all matter is constantly changing. The desires and habits of people change, availability of mortgage money changes, population changes, government decisions change, and many other economic forces are in a continual state of change. These and other factors cause real estate prices and sales velocity to change. Thus, we move from a buyer's to a seller's market and back again.

Since any appraisal is made as of a specific date, reflecting the economic conditions at that point in time, the sale price of any comparable used must be adjusted to reflect the change of market conditions from its sale date to the effective date of appraisal.

The question to be answered here is "how much more or less would the comparable sell for if sold at the effective date of appraisal rather than on the date of its actual sale?"

Only by keeping abreast of the market can an appraiser make a sound judgement as to the necessary adjustments for time.

LOCATION

If the comparable sales are within the same neighbourhood as the subject property, and are similarly zoned, they will likely be competitive and may not require a location adjustment. However, sales in a different neighbourhood may require a large adjustment for locational factors. In making adjustments for location, consideration should be given to:

age and condition

price range and size

zoning

services and amenities

social and economic compatability

The question to be asked here is "how much more or less would a typical buyer pay for the comparable if it were located in the subject neighbourhood?" or if it is located on a corner lot within the subject neighbourhood, "how much more or less would a buyer pay if it were located on a lot identical with the subject's?"

PHYSICAL CHARACTERISTICS

It is highly probable that all comparables will differ from each other and the subject property to some extent—for example, differences in area, garage or parking facilities, aesthetic appeal, extra built-in features, and so on. Thus, an adjustment must be made under this heading for physical differences. This element may be broken down to sub elements for easy comparison and be considered under sub elements as:

style and layout

area or volume

number of rooms or units

age

condition

functional adequacy

site size and improvements

quality of construction

accessory buildings

special features

The question to be asked here is "how much more or less would the buyer have paid for this comparable if its physical characteristics were the same as subject?" This question is best answered by an item by item comparison.

④ MOTIVATING FORCES

This element consists of terms and conditions of the sale. Here we deal with such items as cash payment, interest rates and mortgage amortization term. For example, one comparable may have sold for a very low cash payment with two or three mortgages. Thus, it may have reflected a higher sale price. Further, the buyer may have assumed an existing mortgage with a lower interest rate than can now be acquired.

Other considerations are:

Was it a quick sale for some compelling reason?

Was there a prior relationship between the buyer and seller?

Was the sale arms length?

Was the buyer and / or seller under any pressure to buy or sell?

The question to be asked here is "was the sale arms length and under typical financing for the neighbourhood?"

The Adjustment Process

Having described each comparable sale in sufficient detail, the appraiser then adjusts the sale price of each for differences between it and the subject property. It is important to remember that you always adjust the comparable to the subject property. In this way you reach a conclusion as to what price the comparable would have sold for had it possessed the same characteristics as the subject property. Further, you conclude with an indication of value for the subject property.

Adjustments should only be made for the significant and pertinent characteristics. Further, each lump sum adjustment should be defendable by market data. For example, the market may indicate that the *difference in price* paid for a house with an attached garage as compared to one without a garage is $1,500. notwithstanding that the *cost* of adding the garage may be $2,000. The principle of contribution underlies the entire adjustment process, therefore, it is necessary to consider what difference in price will be paid for a property by the presence or absence of factors being considered.

When a purchaser buys a residence, he buys the entire package, which includes land and building, at a given price. If we were to attempt to analyse the building and assign a value for each part such as the garage, recreation room, extra washroom etc., we might well end up with a higher value than the market will really pay. This is like the restauranteur who buys a pie for $1.00, cuts it into 8 pieces and sells each piece for twenty cents, thereby grossing $1.60. It follows that when making adjustments for different contributing parts of a house, such an adjusted amount must reflect its contribution to the package and not necessary its cost.

As stated earlier, all adjustments are made relative to the subject property, therefore, when making any adjustments the following rules must be adhered to:

1. If the comparable is better than the subject property, make a downward adjustment.

For example: comparable has 2 baths, subject has 1 bath; thus the comparable in this respect is better than the subject, consequently the adjustment is a minus or downward amount.

2. If the comparable is poorer or less desirable than the subject, make an upward adjustment.

For example: if the comparable has an old standard kitchen, and the subject a new modernized one, then in this respect the comparable is inferior, consequently the adjustment is a plus or upward one.

As also mentioned earlier, it is proper to adjust for *time* first, and then total the adjustment and apply that sum to the time adjusted price.

Types of Adjustment

There are two main methods of adjustments used by appraisers. Of the two types, the same type should be employed throughout the adjustment process and should reflect appropriate market reactions in both direction and size. The two methods are as follows:

Plus or Minus dollar adjustment.

Plus or Minus percentage adjustment.

METHOD 1: PLUS OR MINUS DOLLAR ADJUSTMENT

This method is market oriented and therefore reflects the reactions of a typical buyer who, in comparing one property with another, consciously or subconsciously adds or subtracts sums for differences in various properties. Thus, under each heading, a plus or minus dollar sum will appear, which represents the appraiser's best judgement as to what the typical buyer is likely to allow.

METHOD 2: PLUS OR MINUS PERCENTAGE ADJUSTMENT

The net result of both Method 1 and Method 2 is an accumulated dollar or percentage amount ultimately translated to a dollar amount. When precise dollar amounts cannot be estimated from the market, the appraiser will allocate a percentage difference based on his best judgement. This method is less commonly used as it tends to act as a hedge against the allocating of dollar amounts.

Mechanics of the Adjustment Process

ELEMENTS: TIME

This element accounts for any value change from the sale date of the comparable to the effective date of valuation, thereby placing the comparable sale within the same economic market conditions as the subject property. This involves the principle of change and recollection of our earlier studies on trend analysis. In this regard, value trends may be accounted for in two ways:

Real Estate Board Publications. Various real estate boards publish price levels of property each month by the area. This usually shows the average price paid within the given area and any increase or decrease in value over the preceding month from which a percentage of change can be calculated.

Example

You are making an adjustment to one of the comparable sales which sold in December 1981 adjusting same to December 1982. The publication of the average prices for the given area shows that the average price at December 1981 was $150,000.00 and for December 1982 $180,000. Therefore, price increase December 1981 to December 1982 is $30,000.

Percent increase = $30,000.00/$150,000.00 x 100 = 20%

Price increase per month = 20/12 = 1.67%

The foregoing example provides a good rule of thumb check for average increases or decreases. Since, however, the area may cover many neighbourhoods and thereby many markets, the indicated value change may not be accurate for a specific neighbourhood.

Study of Neighbourhood Trends. This method involves making a search for sales and resales of the same property within the neighbourhood of the subject property being appraised. In an active market, this method will most probably produce the best and most accurate trend data for the subject property.

The data from the example and trend analysis on the following page indicate that properties within the subject neighbourhood have increased in value at a range of .9% to 1.3% per month during 1980. This range being reasonably close, the appraiser may conclude that prices increased at the rate of 1% per month during 1982. Once this conclusion is reached, each comparable sale may be adjusted for time accordingly.

It is important to note, however, that the appraiser must make certain that the value appreciation is in fact attributable solely to the passage of time and not to some property improvements. It becomes clear that discussions should be held with the vendor to clarify this particular point.

Example

The neighbourhood search will produce say 30 sales between January and December of the year 1982. Of these 30 sales, you find that 3 were resold within the same year.

Sale 1: sold April 1982 at $150,000.00
         resold October 1982 at $162,000.00

Sale 12: sold May 1982 at $153,500.00
         resold December 1982 at $164,200.00

Sale 23: sold January 1982 at $148,000.00
         resold December 1982 at $162,800.00

Method of Trend Analysis

Sale No.	1	12	23
Date of Sale	April, 1982	May, 1982	Jan. 1982
Sale Price	$150,000	$153,500	$148,000
Date of Resale	Oct. 1982	Dec. 1982	Dec. 1982
Resale Price	$162,000	$164,200	$162,800
Time Difference	6 months	7 months	11 months
Price Increase	$12,000	$10,700	$14,800
% Increase	$\frac{12,000}{150,000} = .08$	$\frac{10,700}{153,500} = .07$	$\frac{14,800}{148,000} = .10$
% Increase/ Month	.08/6 = .013	.07/7 = .01	.10/11 = .009

Indicated increase (approx.) 1% per month

LOCATION

This element accounts for locational obsolescence or the difference in price that a purchaser may pay due to (1) neighbourhood characteristics, where the comparable is located in a different neighbourhood than subject; or (2) location within the block, where the comparable may be a corner location and the subject an inside lot.

1. Differing Neighbourhood Characteristics. Where the comparable is in a different neighbourhood, the question to be answered is "are buyers paying more for houses in the comparable neighbourhood than in the subject neighbourhood?" To answer this question, the appraiser must make a study of each neighbourhood to note the general price levels being paid for houses comparable to subject. To refine the method, the sale price should be reduced to some unit of comparison, say the sale price per square metre of building, including land, for all sales in both neighbourhoods. It may be found that the range of per unit value is the same, more or less, for both neighbourhoods. In this case, no adjustment would be made. On the other hand, if the range for the comparable neighbourhood centered about $300.00 per square metre and for the subject neighbourhood $330.00 per square metre, then it follows that the comparable is 10% inferior to the subject neighbourhood, and an upward of plus 10% adjustment is required. **Method of Calculation:** 30/300 x 100 = 10%.

2. Differing Block Locations. If the comparable is a corner lot and the subject property an inside lot, the question to be answered is "which location provides the greatest amenity features, and does the typical buyer make an allowance for this in the price he pays?" To answer this question, the appraiser must analyze the comparable sales, noting the prices paid for similar houses on corner lots as compared to prices paid for houses on inside lots. If the market indicates that houses on corner lots sell at $50,000.00 and the same house on an inside lot sells at $55,000.00, corner lots would appear to be inferior by 10%, and an upward or plus adjustment of 10% required. **Method of Calculation:** 5,000/50,000 x 100 = 10%

PHYSICAL CHARACTERISTICS

As discussed in the earlier part of the Direct Sales Comparison Approach theory, adjustments for this element may be refined by considering the differences under sub element headings such as landscaping, garage, recreation room, washroom, extra equipment, etc. It should be remembered, however, the reproduction cost of such differences is not necessarily the measure of the difference in price that a purchaser would pay for the item itself. The true measure is the extra amount a typical buyer would be likely to pay for it as part of the package.

Example

Suppose that the comparable has an attached garage, and the subject property has no garage. An analysis of sales will indicate that houses with garages sell at higher prices than similar houses without a garage. This same rule will probably apply to other physical features and adjustments will be required for these differences. Thus, if the sale is comparable to the subject property in all respects except for the added feature of an attached garage, and the amount indicates that garages add $1,500.00 to the sale price, then the adjustment for this sale would be $1,500.00.

Each item of difference is treated in a like manner and their sum represents the amount of adjustment for physical attributes. Another thing which should be borne in mind is the imperfection of the market. In the previous example, there may be a mathematical difference of $1,500.00, however the appraiser must judge whether this amount is due to the presence of the garage, to the market imperfection, or to both.

MOTIVATION

This element deals primarily with two factors: (1) whether the sale is an arms length one or to a relative, etc.; and (2) whether or not the financing is typical of the neighbourhood.

1. **Arms Length Factor.** The appraiser can determine if the sale is bonafide when he confirms it with one of the principals to the sale. Should he find that the sale was transacted in a hurry, or that either the buyer or seller was a better negotiator, or that either buyer or seller was not properly informed as to the going price, he must make the proper adjustment based on this information. **For example, if the sale was from brother to sister and the market indicates that the price was low by $2,000.00, an upward adjustment of this amount should be made.**

2. **Financing.** The comparable sale may not have been transacted under typical financing conditions. **For example:** The owner may have accepted a low cash payment and held the first mortgage for the balance; it may have been an all cash sale at a time when a purchaser would have found it difficult to arrange financing; or there may have been an existing mortgage of 10% whereas the current rate is 15%. In the first case, the price may have been $3,000.00 more than the market would bear because of the purchaser's low equity. Thus a downward adjustment of this amount may be required. In the second case, the sale price may have been lower than market by $2,000.00 due to the all cash arrangement sought by the seller and an upward adjustment of this amount should be made. In the third case, the lower interest rate may have been both beneficial and desirable to the purchaser, inducing him to pay more in view of the interest savings he would make over the mortgage term remaining. Such savings would be the present worth of the difference in interest payments over the balance of the mortgage term.

Remarks. In an active market, comparable sales requiring this element of adjustment may be discarded entirely because of the many other sales available. However, if sufficient comparables with typical financing are not available and adjustments have to be made to the comparable for financing, this can be done quite simply with the use of published mortgage value tables.

YIELD TABLE

$\left\{\begin{array}{l}\text{DISCOUNTED MORTGAGE EVALUATION}\\ \text{PER \$1000 OUTSTANDING PRINCIPAL}\end{array}\right.$

	12% ANNUAL RATE						25 YRS AMORTIZATION			

REMAINING TERM IN YEARS

YIELD RATE	1	2	3	4	5	6	7	8	9	10
8.00	1036	1070	1101	1129	1155	1178	1200	1220	1237	1253
8.50	1032	1061	1087	1112	1134	1154	1172	1189	1204	1217
9.00	1027	1052	1074	1095	1113	1130	1145	1159	1171	1182
9.50	1022	1043	1061	1078	1093	1107	1119	1130	1140	1148
10.00	1018	1034	1049	1062	1073	1084	1094	1102	1109	1116
10.25	1015	1029	1042	1054	1064	1073	1081	1088	1095	1101
10.50	1013	1025	1036	1046	1054	1062	1069	1075	1080	1085
10.75	1011	1021	1030	1038	1045	1051	1057	1062	1066	1070
11.00	1008	1016	1024	1030	1036	1041	1045	1049	1052	1055
11.25	1006	1012	1018	1022	1026	1030	1033	1036	1039	1041
11.50	1004	1008	1011	1015	1017	1020	1022	1024	1025	1027
11.75	1002	1004	1005	1007	1008	1010	1011	1012	1012	1013
12.00	1000	1000	1000	1000	1000	1000	1000	1000	1000	1000
12.25	997	995	994	992	991	990	989	988	987	986
12.50	995	991	988	985	982	980	978	976	974	973
12.75	993	987	982	977	973	970	967	965	962	960
13.00	991	983	976	970	965	961	957	953	950	948
13.25	988	979	970	963	957	951	946	942	939	935
13.50	986	975	965	956	948	942	936	931	927	923
13.75	984	971	959	949	940	933	926	921	916	912
14.00	982	967	953	942	932	924	916	910	905	900
14.25	980	963	948	935	924	915	907	900	894	889
14.50	978	959	942	928	916	906	897	889	883	877
14.75	975	955	937	922	908	897	888	879	872	866
15.00	973	951	931	915	901	889	878	870	862	856
15.25	971	947	926	908	893	880	869	860	852	845
15.50	969	943	921	902	886	872	860	850	842	835
15.75	967	939	915	895	878	864	851	841	832	825
16.00	965	935	910	889	871	855	843	832	822	815
16.25	963	931	905	882	863	847	834	822	813	805
16.50	961	928	900	876	856	839	825	814	804	795
16.75	958	924	895	870	849	832	817	805	794	786
17.00	956	920	889	864	842	824	809	796	785	777
17.25	954	916	884	858	835	816	801	788	777	768
17.50	952	913	879	852	828	809	793	779	768	759
17.75	950	909	874	846	821	801	785	771	759	750
18.00	948	905	869	840	815	794	777	763	751	741
18.25	946	902	865	834	808	787	769	755	743	733
18.50	944	898	860	828	801	780	762	747	735	725
18.75	942	894	855	822	795	773	754	739	727	717
19.00	940	891	850	816	789	766	747	731	719	709
19.25	938	887	845	811	782	759	740	724	711	701
19.50	936	884	840	805	776	752	733	717	704	693
19.75	934	880	836	799	770	745	725	709	696	685
20.00	932	877	831	794	764	739	719	702	689	678

Example

A vendor has taken back a mortgage of $40,000 with an interest rate of 12% per annum calculated semi-annually not in advance. The mortgage is to run for a five-year term and has blended monthly payments amortized over 25 years. The current rate of interest on this type of mortgage is 18%. How much would the appraiser have to adjust this sale to reflect the unusual beneficial financing? The tables demonstrate that to yield 18% over 5 years an investor could afford to pay $815 per thousand for this mortgage: $815 x 40 = $32,600. The amount of the adjustment therefore is:

$$\$40{,}000 - \$32{,}600 = \$7{,}400$$

Such yield tables can be used to calculate the adjustment on any mortgage provided the appraiser is aware of the term, amortization period and interest rate. These tables, which are available from various publishers may be used to calculate the discount (or the adjustment) required on a mortgage that has already been in

134   Principles of Appraisal

existence for several years. In such a case, however, it is the *remaining* term and amortization period that should be considered in calculating the discount.

Presentation of the Adjustment Process

1. Provide a detailed narrative of each comparable sale so that the reader of the report can understand the adjustments made.
2. Reduce the sale price to the appropriate unit of comparison.
3. Justify each adjustment in narrative form, from market evidence.
4. Prepare an adjustment grid in tabular form.

Example of Adjustment Process—Single Family Residence
Date of valuation: April 20, 1981

Comparable Sale No. 3
- sold Dec. 18, 1980 at $52,000.
- market data indicates price increase of 3% per month during past year.
- comparable has 6 rooms, 2 baths and superior landscaping, but no garage
- subject property has 1 attached garage, 6 rooms, 1 bath
- sale was arms length
The market indicates that an attached garage adds $1,500, extra bath $1,700, landscaping $650.
- inferior location $800.00

Item	Comparable Sale No. 3
Sale Price	$52,000
Time Adjustment	+ 6,240
Time Adjusted Price	$58,240
Other Adjustments:	
Location	+ 800
Garage	+ 1,500
Bath	− 1,700
Landscaping	− 650
Total Other Adjustments	− 50
Indicated Value of Subject	$58,190

Figure 15 (on the following page) illustrates this adjustment process in tabular form using 6 comparable properties. The only difference is that the items are listed horizontally instead of vertically.

Figure 15

Comparable Sales Adjustment Chart—Single Family Dwelling
Adjustments

Sale No.	Date of Sale	Selling Price	Time	Time Adj. Price	Location	Lot Size	Land-Scaping	Bldg. Size	Condition	Special Features	Garage	Total Adj.	Adj. Price Subj.
1	3/76	52,500	—	—	—	—	+600	—	+600	—	—	+1,200	53,700
2	9/75	56,400	+1,410	57,810	-1,500	—	-300	—	—	-1,000	—	-2,800	55,010
3	1/76	48,600	+400	49,000	+1,500	—	+600	—	-600	—	+2,700	+4,200	53,200
4	9/75	53,700	+1,340	55,040	—	+600	—	-900	-1,000	—	—	-1,300	53,740
5	11/75	54,000	+875	54,875	—	+900	—	-1,800	—	—	—	-900	53,975
6	3/76	54,800	—	—	-900	—	-300	—	—	—	—	-1,200	53,600

Reconciliation

Sales No. 1 and No. 6 have the least number of adjustments and are most comparable. They have been given the greatest weight, but are reasonably supported by the other comparable sales.

Final Estimate of Value by the Direct Sales Comparison Approach—$53,700.00.

Market evaluation for income property.

Basic Units, The Apartment Building

If sufficient data is available, the Direct Sales Comparison Approach is usually more convincing than the other two approaches. With this type of property, basic units of comparison are as follows:

- sale price per room
- rooms per apartment
- rental per room per month
- gross rent multiple
- sale price per apartment

The comparison chart may appear as follows:

Item	Comparable Sale No. 2	Subject
No. of Storeys	4	4
Units	24	20
Rooms	96	80
Age	12 yrs.	11 yrs.
Sale Price	$600,000.00	?
Annual Gross Rent	$120,000.00	$99,000.00

The rating grid may appear as follows:

Item	Comparable Sale No. 2	Subject
Rooms per apt.	4	4
Rental/room/month	$104.17	$103.13
Sale price per room	$6,250.00	?
Gross Rent Multiple	5	
Sale price per unit	$25,000.00	

In actual practice, three or four good comparables should be used and set out according to the above rating grid or one designed for your purpose. From this information, a range of unit value indicators will result which can be applied to the subject property. For example, Sale 2 above indicates that this type of building:

sells within the range of $6,250.00 per room

sells within the range of $25,000.00 per unit

rents for $104.17 per room

sells for approximately 5 times the gross income

Applying these data to the subject property would indicate a value as follows:

80 rooms x $6,250.00 = $500,000.00

20 units at $25,000.00 = $500,000.00

5 x $99,000.00 = $495,000.00

RATIONALE

In order for sales to be comparable, similarity must exist as to location, age of building, leases, expenses, and condition of building, financing, vacancy rate and management. In the real marketplace, indications will not be as pat as shown above. Assuming all of the above factors are comparable, the gross rent multiplier should not be underrated.

Commercial and Industrial Property

GENERAL

As long as sufficient market data are available, the Direct Sale Comparison Approach can be applied to commercial and industrial property in essentially the same way as for residential property. The main differences are in the consideration of the rent producing capacities of both the subject and the comparable sales with regard to the quantity, quality and durability of the rental income.

Recorded as well as non-recorded leases may be used. With regard to lease data, it is important to consider the date upon which the leases were executed and the terms of the leases. Leases generally vary regarding terms. For example, rentals cannot be compared without clarifying details such as who pays heat, utilities, taxes, insurance and maintenance, etc. The rate charged for modern office space, for example, may include all services, taxes and heat; the tenant of a store, however, may, in addition to his rent, be required to pay heat, light, water and tax escalation.

The length of the lease is also important. Where, for example, a lease is signed for 5 to 10 years, the owner is assured of continued occupancy and income for this period. However, if the market is fast rising, the owner cannot share in value increases as rents increase during the lease term. Thus the tenant's leasehold interest gains in value. Also rents may be more conservative if the tenant has a good financial rating and leases for a long term.

RETAIL STORE

Here, leases are the first concern due to the usual single occupancy. Fly-by-night tenants are the cause of higher than usual vacancy rates causing a lower net income even if the short term rents are high. Thus a more conservative rent to a financially strong tenant is better than a high short term rent with two to four months of vacancies per year.

Buyers of stores are of two types—investment purchasers, or owner occupants. Typical buyers of stores are not usually sophisticated investors such as the purchasers of large shopping centres, major office buildings and the like. Thus, they are not usually acquainted with the complexities of the income approach and most often use a rule of thumb method such as the gross rent multiplier. In other words, they buy at some multiple of gross annual rent.

Stores vary in age, location and condition. Usually older stores require greater maintenance and are due for major capital expenses such as new roof, furnace, wiring, etc. Thus, maintenance and repair costs are higher than with new stores that have many years of income before capital expenditures are required. Further, older stores generally rent for a lesser amount than newer stores. The end result is that the owner of an older store may be left with less net income.

Example—Two Stores of Equal Size		
Item	*New Store*	*Old Store*
Gross Rent	$26,875.00	$20,000.00
Operating Expenses	8,062.00	8,000.00
Net Income	$18,813.00	$12,000.00

Typical buyers generally pay prices ranging from 5 to 8 times gross income. For example, a new store in a 100% corner location may sell at 8 times gross or, in this case, $215,000.00 ($26,875.00 x 8). The same store on the shopping periphery may sell at 5.58 times gross income, or $150,000.00 ($26,875.00 x 5.58). Older stores may sell at 4 to 6 times gross depending on the desirability of their location.

In order to estimate the correct multiple to be used, a market study of all sales and rentals must be carried out for the neighbourhood. This information is then set up in grid form from which an analysis and conclusion can be reached as to the proper gross rent multiple to use.

SHOPPING CENTRES

It is usually difficult, if not impossible to acquire all pertinent data on this type of property necessary to process a proper income approach report. Owners of shopping centres are usually quite secretive about their income and expenses not only with appraisers but also with each other. Consequently, each owner usually operates his centre without the benefit of pooled information from other owners. The appraiser can usually find the sale price and the gross rents, however. From these data he can estimate the gross rent multiplier and apply it just as in the case of retail store appraisal.

INDUSTRIAL

This type of property comes in many forms. There is the light industry, heavy industry, single and multi-storey, and plaza type. Comparable sales should be representative of the type of property being appraised. For example, in appraising a single storey light industrial plant, one uses comparables of this kind. The sale price is usually broken down to a square metre rate for the building including the land. For example:

sale price: $250,000.00

gross floor area: 930 square metres

sale price per square metre of building including land (approx.) $270.

When selecting comparables care must be taken to ensure that those selected have the same building to land ratio as that of the subject. Should a sale contain extra land, it may be necessary to deduct the contributing amount in the adjustment process to account for it. Other conditions to be considered are: age, quality of construction, location, extra fixtures and equipment, ratio of office to plant space, etc.

Advantages and Disadvantages of the Direct Sales Comparison Approach

Advantages

It reflects market behaviour.

It is widely used and understood.

It is accorded greatest weight by the courts.

It requires least adjustment if sufficient data are available.

Disadvantages

If inadequate data are available, it may be impossible to apply.

Adjustments must be made—no two properties are ever identical.

Sales are always historical.

Accuracy of the method depends on appraiser's ability to recognize differences.

It is sometimes difficult to ascertain circumstances surrounding a sale.

Summary

The Direct Sales Comparison Approach is based primarily on the Principle of Substitution. The informed purchaser would pay no more for a property than the cost of obtaining a comparable, competitive property with the same utility, on the open market, provided there is no undue delay in making the acquisition.

The best results from this approach are obtained when good and truly comparable properties are used. The best comparables are those which require the least amount of adjustment. The best comparison can be made when the selling price is reduced to a proper unit of comparison. Adjustments are then made to the sale price per unit. It is always best to make any necessary time adjustment first, then apply the total of all other adjustments to the time adjusted price per unit to arrive at a fully adjusted price per unit from each comparable.

The final step in the approach is to reconcile these indicated selling prices into one final estimate of value by this approach.

Chapter 7

Step Seven
Reconciliation of Value Indications
and Final Estimate

Reconciliation

We have now come to the point where the appraiser has completed the approaches relevant to the subject property and is faced with the inevitable variance in the value estimated by the various methods. At this critical point, the appraiser must reconcile the estimates and decide on the final estimate of value.

The term "Reconciliation" need not strike fear in the heart of the budding appraiser. Reconciliation is defined as the process by which the appraiser evaluates and selects from among two or more alternative conclusions or indications to reach a single value estimate. Present appraisal practice requires the appraiser to indicate only one value figure for his Final Estimate of market value and the various values indicated by the approaches must be reviewed with this purpose in mind.

In the reconciliation, the appraiser reviews the reliability of the data used in each approach and weigh their relevance to the property being appraised. The most weight is given to the best and most reliable data and *method* for the type and class of property, and based on the appraiser's judgement and experience, a final estimate of value is arrived at.

It is important to emphasize that the reconciliation process is not simply a method of averaging the estimates of the approaches used, as this denies common sense and judgement. In considering the relevance of the methods used, the appraiser must bear in mind the advantages and disadvantages of each approach.

The Cost Approach

ADVANTAGES

People understand it.

It is often the only method to use in the appraisal of special purpose properties.

There is relative ease in making a cost calculation.

DISADVANTAGES

It is difficult to estimate depreciation, particularly in older buildings.

While the cost of construction appears relatively easy to estimate, there is no exact cost figure. Several methods yield varying costs.

Construction costs are constantly changing.

The Income Approach

ADVANTAGES

It is particularly applicable in estimating the value of income producing or investment properties.

DISADVANTAGES

The major problem with the Income Approach is the difficulty of selecting an appropriate capitalization rate.

Estimating the income and the operating expenses can sometimes prove difficult, and a slight error in either estimate is magnified on capitalization.

It is of no use in the appraisal of owner-occupied and/or special purpose properties.

The Direct Sales Comparison Approach

ADVANTAGES

People understand it and use it.

It gets around the problems of estimating costs, depreciation, rentals and expenses.

It is generally accepted by courts, boards and the general public.

DISADVANTAGES

It is sometimes difficult to obtain good comparable sales.

Making adjustments for differences requires careful judgement and experience and these adjustments are often difficult to support and explain satisfactorily.

It is often difficult to obtain all the relevant information relating to each sale, particularly with reference to motivation.

The data are historical in nature.

After giving consideration to the reliability of the evidence presented in each of the approaches used, and giving the most weight to that approach which has the most reliable data, the appraiser selects the final estimate of value and proceeds to write the report.

Reconciliation Example

The value estimates, as developed in detail in this report, have resulted in the following:

Cost Approach	$82,500
The Direct Sales Comparison Approach	$81,000

The Cost Approach contains a land value estimate which is well supported and considered sound. However estimates of current reproduction cost and accrued depreciation of a fifteen year old building are very difficult to make and to support. For this reason, the value indicated by this approach has been given the least weight.

The Direct Sales Comparison Approach reflects the current thinking of buyers and sellers in the market place for this type of property. A desirable situation existed here in that the comparables were recent sales requiring very little adjustment. Furthermore, the quality of the data left no question as to its reliability. Bearing in mind the purpose and the function of this appraisal, this approach to value is deemed to have the greatest significance in the final estimate of value.

The estimated market value of the subject property as of December 31, 1982 is:

EIGHTY-ONE THOUSAND DOLLARS
($81,000.00)

The Appraisal Report

The minimum contents of any appraisal report should be as follows:

1. An adequate description of the property being appraised.

2. The purpose of the appraisal and a definition of the value estimate.

3. The effective date of the appraisal.

4. A statement of the estimated Highest and Best Use of the subject property.

5. Reasoning supporting the value conclusion together with such data as may be considered necessary within the scope of the assignment.

6. The final estimate of value.

7. Special and limiting conditions, if any.

8. The appraiser's certification and signature.

The Limiting Conditions are usually included in every report to set the framework upon which the appraisal is based. A typical statement of Limiting Conditions might contain the following:

1. The legal description as shown is assumed to be correct.

2. No responsibility is assumed for matters legal in nature, nor is an opinion rendered as to the title, which is assumed to be good.

3. The sketches in this report are included to assist the reader in visualizing the property, however, as no survey of the property was available, information relating to the size and area was obtained from the deed and assessment records. Should a survey show dimensions and area other than stated herein, the opinion of value may have to be altered.

4. Possession of this report or a copy thereof does not carry with the right of publication, nor may it be used for any purpose by other than the applicant without the previous written consent of the appraiser.

5. The appraiser is not required to give testimony or attendance in court by reason of this appraisal unless arrangements have been previously made therefor.

6. The distribution of the total valuation in this report between land and improvements applies only under the existing program of utilization. The separate valuation for land and buildings must not be used in conjunction with any other appraisal and are invalid if so used.

Certification by the Appraiser

Included in the appraisal report should be a certification signed by the appraiser. This certification usually reads as follows:

I hereby certify that I have personally inspected the property appraised and that I have no present or contemplated interest therein.

Neither the employment to make this appraisal nor the compensation paid is contingent on the amount of the valuation reported.

_____

Signature of Appraiser

Types of Appraisal Reports

There are three basic type of reports:

1. The Form Report
2. The Letter of Opinion
3. The Full Narrative Report

The Form Report is usually prepared by appraisers who are employees of institutions and government agencies and who are making internal reports for their organizations. The advantages of the Form Report are that only the bare essentials are included. The standard form makes it easy for the reader to locate specific information and it enables the appraiser to complete the report rapidly. The form usually contains space to quickly check off the various types of construction, interior details and locational information. Space is provided for a routine appraisal method, and in some reports a section is also included for a brief sketch and a photograph.

The Letter of Opinion is usually a brief statement of the appraiser's estimate of value, which in many cases is all that the client requires. It is most important, however, for the appraiser to retain all his supporting research should it be required at a later date, and a statement to this effect is sometimes included in the letter. It must be strongly emphasized that a Letter of Opinion report does not absolve the appraiser from doing all the work required to estimate the Market Value as carefully and accurately as possible. The same amount of research is required whether the appraiser is providing a client with a Letter of Opinion or a Full Narrative Report.

The Narrative Report is a full report which describes in greater detail the regional and neighbourhood analysis, a full description and identification of the property and the methods and reasoning used in arriving at the estimate of value. This report is often used for presentation to courts and boards in cases of expropriation, and/or for presentation to clients who are not familiar with the area or the property. It leads the reader through the logically related steps to the final estimate of value. Its purpose, of course, is to draw the reader along, presenting him with the evidence the appraiser has collected and presented so that the reader is fully convinced and satisfied when the final estimate of value is reached.

Regardless of the type of report used, it should be evident that an appraisal report is a permanent graphic presentation of the appraiser's work and it should, therefore, be prepared and presented in the best professional tradition. The appraiser should endeavour to insure that the typing, sketches and photographs are carefully done, that the report is presented in an attractive cover, and that where possible, colour is used to emphasize important details and provide variety. Examples of the three types of report follow as an Appendix to this Chapter.

Summary

Reconciliation is a process of logical analysis whereby a basis for selection among alternative results or conclusions is developed. While it is applied throughout the entire appraisal framework, it is especially important in selecting a final value estimate from among two or more indications of value obtained through alternative approaches to value estimation.

Prior to Final Reconciliation of Value Indicators into a Final Estimate of Value, the appraiser should review all data, analysis and calculations in all the approaches used.

The final value estimate represents the appraiser's professional opinion of the value of the subject property, consistent with the definition of value being sought; the quantity and quality of available data; and the applicability of the underlying theory of the several approaches to value estimation to the problem at hand.

The appraisal report is a written presentation of the general and specific data considered and analysed, the methods used, the techniques employed together with reconciliation that leads to the final estimate of value. The report should be prepared and documented in such a manner as to lead the reader to the same conclusions arrived at by the appraiser.

Appendix to Chapter Seven

The Form Report
The Letter of Opinion
The Narrative Report

RESIDENTIAL
APPRAISAL REPORT

FOR: NAME: Mr. John C. Hopeful   DATE: December 15, 19X0

ADDRESS: 4360 Mancroft Crescent   PHONE: 376-4215

CITY/TOWN: REXDALE, Ontario

ATTENTION:

PURPOSE OF APPRAISAL: To estimate the market value of the subject property as of November 30, 19X0.

GENERAL

OWNERSHIP: Fee Simple

Property's Civic Address	Legal Description — Lot, Plan, Township, County.
4360 Mancroft Crescent, Rexdale	Lot 332, Plan M1836, Etobicoke

Municipality: Etobicoke

Zoning	Annual Taxes	Total Assessed Value	Age of Dwelling
Single Family Residence (R-2)	$1,048 for yr X0	$6,150	☐ New 15 Yrs.

Describe any unusual easements, restrictions or rights of way.

NEIGHBOURHOOD

Class	Trend	Type	Age	Area Is Built Up	Distance to Schools
☐ Excellent	☐ Improving	☒ Single Family ☐ Industrial	☐ New	☒ 100%	Elementary 2 blocks
☒ Good	☒ Stable	☐ Multi-Family ☐ Mixed	☐ 1 to 10 yrs.	☐ 75%	Secondary 6 blocks
☐ Fair	☐ Declining	☐ Commercial ☐ Undeveloped	☒ 11 to 30 yrs.	☐ 50%	Shopping 4 blocks
☐ Poor	☐	☐	☐ Over 30 yrs.	☐ 25%	Public Transit 1 block
					Recreational Fac. 4 blocks

Services & Utilities			Dwelling for Area	Adjoining Homes	Subject to Flood Hazard	Highest & Best Use
Road	☒ Paved	☐ Unpaved			☒ No	Present ☒
Drainage	☒ Sewer	☐ Septic	☒ Comparable	☐ Smaller	☐ Yes	or
Water Supply	☒ Municipal	☐ Well	☐ Superior	☒ Similar		
Electric ☒	Gas ☒	Telephone ☒	☐ Inferior	☐ Larger		

DESCRIPTION OF IMPROVEMENTS

EXTERIOR

Family Units	Building Type	Foundation	Exterior Walls	Roof	Parking	Garage
☒ Single	☐ Bung. ☒ Detached	☐ Poured Concrete	☒ Brick Veneer	☒ Asphalt Shingle	☐ Lane	☐ Attached
☐ Duplex	☐ S/L ☐ Semi-Detached	☒ Concrete Blocks	☐ Solid Brick	☐ Wood Shingle	☒ Private Drive	☐ Detached
☐ Triplex	☐ 1 1/2 ☐ Attached	☐ Other	☐ Stucco	or Shake	☐ Mutual Drive	☐ Built-in
☐ Other	☒ 2 ☐ Condominium		☐ Aluminium Siding	☐ Built-Up	☐ None	☐ Car Port
		Framing	☒ Clapboard	Tar & Gravel	☐ On Street	☒ Non
	Age of building	☒ Wood		☐ Slate	☐	No. of Cars
		☐ Steel		☐ Metal		1 2 3
		☐ Other				☐ ☐ ☐

INTERIOR

Basement	Framing	Heating System	Insulation	Electric Wiring	Plumbing
☒ Full	☐ Masonry	☒ Forced Air Ducted ☐ Hot Water	☒ Adequate	☐ 200 Amp. Service	Fixtures ☒ Average ☐ Above Average
☐ Partial	☐ Steel	☐ Gravity ☐	☐ Deficient	☒ 100 Amp. Service	Piping ☒ Copper ☐ Plastic
☐ Crawl	☒ Wood	☐ Electric		☐ 60 Amp. Service	☐ Galvanized ☐ Other
☐ None	☐			☐	Laundry Tubs ☒ Yes

Fireplace 1 2	Floor Plan	Exterior Condition (For Age)	Interior Condition (For Age)
☐ Yes ☐ ☐ ☒ No	☒ Satisfactory	☐ Excellent	☐ Excellent
	☐ Unsatisfactory	☒ Good	☒ Good

Interior Walls		Floors		
☒ Drywall	☐ Plywood	☒ Hardwood	☐ Satisfactory	☐ Satisfactory
☐ Lath and Plaster ☐		☐ Vinyl Tile	☐ Poor (explain below)	☐ Poor (Explain below)
☐ Panelling ☐		☒ Broadloom		

Summary of Condition: Average to above average

NUMBER and TYPE of ROOMS									COMMENTS
	L/R	D/R	K	B/R	BATH	WASH	FAM.	OTHER	
Basement								Rec. Rm.	
1st Floor	x	x	x			x			
2nd Floor				4	x				
Other									

KITCHEN	BATHROOM	LIVINGROOM	BEDROOMS	CLOSETS		SPECIAL FEATURES & EQUIPMENT:
Excellent	New	Excellent	Large	Ample		
Good x	Average x	Good x	Medium x	Adequate x		
Fair	Fair	-Fair	Small	Fair		
Poor	Outdated	Poor		Inadequate		

GENERAL COMMENTS

COST APPROACH (IF APPLICABLE)

LAND DIMENSIONS AND VALUE

FRONTAGE	Depth	Area	Rate	
15.24 m	x 37.34 m	= 569.06 m²	x $3615/f.m.	= $55,093.

LAND VALUE (ROUNDED)
$ 55,000.

BUILDINGS

Width	Depth	Area	Rate	Value
8.61 m.	x 8.23 m.	= (70.86)2 m²	x 306.87/m²	= $43,500.
	x	=	x	=
	x	=	x	=
	x	=	x	=

Garage

	x	=	x	= $

TOTAL =. $43,500.
Less Depreciation 36 % $15,660.
Depreciated Cost $27,840.

DEPRECIATED REPRODUCTION COST
$ 27,840.

OTHER IMPROVEMENTS
Description   Depreciated Value

Outside improvements including
driveway, sidewalks, patio and   1,200
landscaping

OTHER IMPROVEMENTS
$ 1,200.

FINAL VALUE ESTIMATE COST APPROACH
$ 84,000.

DIRECT SALES COMPARISON APPROACH

Address:	Date of Sale	Sale price	Lot Size	Bldg. Size	No. Rooms Area/Bedroom/Bath	COMPARABILITY TO SUBJECT: Similar	Superior	Inferior
876 Kearney Dr.	30-10-X0	$ 79,000.	15 x 33 m	145 m².	7-4-1½	☒	☐	☐
697 Moonvalley Dr.	15-11-X0	$ 79,900.	14 x 37 m	143.5 m²	7-4-1	☒	☐	☐
1376 Westhumber Blvd.	8-11-X0	$ 78,250.	15 x 38 m	140.25 m²	7-4-1½	☐	☐	☒
3001 Pergola Rd.	1-11-X0	$ 77,900.	14 x 35 m	141.5 m²	7-4-1	☐	☐	☒
		$				☐	☐	☐

ANALYSIS

No adjustment considered necessary for time - all sales were within two months
of the effective date of appraisal

Minor adjustments were necessary for physical features such as condition of
property, extra washroom, lack of air-conditioning, etc.

ESTIMATED VALUE OF SUBJECT PROPERTY BASED ON THESE SALES

FINAL VALUE ESTIMATE DIRECT SALES COMPARISON APPROACH
$ 80,400.

GENERAL COMMENTS
(Including Negative Features)

The value estimate indicated by the Direct Sales Comparison Approach was given

the greatest weight since it reflected the actions of buyers and sellers of

this type of property in this area.

APPRAISER'S CERTIFICATE

I hereby certify that I have inspected the above mentioned property on _December 5, 19 X0_
to estimate market value of the subject property with improvements in their present state.
    Market value in such context would be defined as "The probable price at which property would sell for
at the date of appraisal allowing a reasonable time to find a purchaser."
    No responsibility has been assumed for matters which are legal in nature, nor has any opinion on title
been rendered, this appraisal assuming marketable title.
    To the best of my knowledge and belief, the statements contained in this appraisal are correct, subject
to the limiting conditions herein set forth.
    Employment in and compensation for making this report are in no way contingent upon the value repor-
ted. I further certify that I have no interest, present or contemplated, in the property appraised.
    As a result of my appraisal and analysis it is my opinion that the market value of the subject property
as at

November 30, 19 X0 is: _Eighty thousand four hundred_ ($ 80,400.)
(Date)   Dollars

December 15 19 X0
(Date)   (Signature of Appraiser)

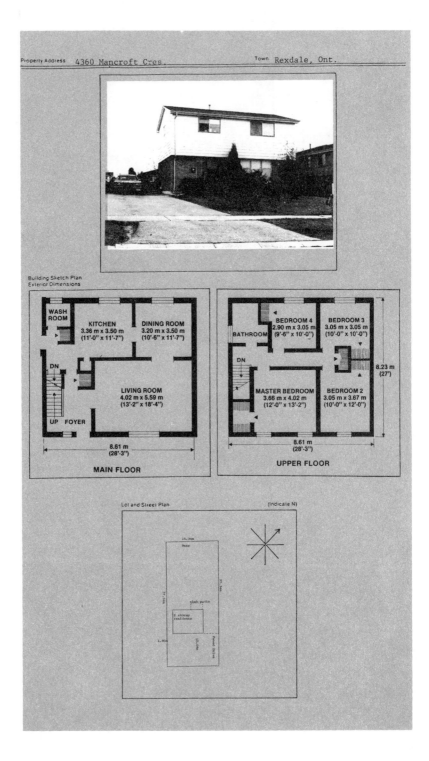

Building Sketch Plan
Exterior Dimensions

MAIN FLOOR

WASH ROOM		
	KITCHEN 3.36 m x 3.50 m (11'-0" x 11'-7")	DINING ROOM 3.20 m x 3.50 m (10'-6" x 11'-7")
DN		LIVING ROOM 4.02 m x 5.59 m (13'-2" x 18'-4")
UP FOYER		

8.81 m
(28'-3")

UPPER FLOOR

BATHROOM BEDROOM 4 2.90 m x 3.05 m (9'-6" x 10'-0") BEDROOM 3 3.05 m x 3.05 m (10'-0" x 10'-0")

DN MASTER BEDROOM 3.66 m x 4.02 m (12'-0" x 13'-2") BEDROOM 2 3.05 m x 3.67 m (10'-0" x 12'-0")

8.23 m (27')

8.61 m (28'-3")

Lot and Street Plan   (Indicate N)

15.34m
Rear

27.34m

27.34m

slab patio

2 storey residence

1.80m

12.18m   Paved Drive

XYZ Appraisals Ltd.
436 The Kingsway
Islington, Ontario

December 15, 1980

Mr. John C. Hopeful
4360 Mancroft Crescent
Rexdale, Ontario

Dear Sir:

Re: Appraisal of 4360 Mancroft Crescent

In compliance with your request for a letter of opinion
as to the value of your property at 4360 Mancroft
Crescent, Rexdale, I wish to advise that I have made a
careful and personal inspection of this residential
site and its building improvements and that I have used
the direct sales comparison approach in estimating its
value.

The purpose of this appraisal was to estimate the
market value of the subject property as of November 30,
1980. "Market value is defined as the probable price
that a property will sell for on the date of appraisal,
allowing a reasonable time to find a purchaser."

The subject property is located in a 15 year old
neighbourhood which is now fully developed with single-
family homes and a few multiple dwellings. Prices of
homes in this area range from a low of about $70,000 to
a high of about $100,000. There are adequate shopping
facilities nearby, and transportation facilities are
excellent.

The site is located on the north side of Mancroft
Crescent, between Jeffcoat Drive and Kearney Drive. It
has a frontage of 15.24 metres by a depth of 37.34
metres including a private paved double driveway. The
improvements on the site consist of a 15 year old brick
veneer, two storey, single-family detached residence
with a living area of approximately 141.72 square
metres.

The ground floor of the residence comprises a vestibule, a good size living room, a family size dining
room, a modern kitchen and a 2-piece washroom. On the
second floor there are four bedrooms and a 4-piece
bathroom. The house has a full basement with a finished recreation room. The building has been well
maintained and as a result it is in a better than
average condition.

In arriving at an estimate of its market value, comparison was made with four similar properties that had
recently sold in this same neighbourhood. These
comparable sales were:

876 Kearney Drive - sold October 30, 1980 for $79,000
697 Moonvalley Drive - sold November 15, 1980 for
                                          $79,900
136 Westhumber Blvd. - sold November 18, 1980 for
                                          $78,250
3001 Pergola Road   - sold November 1, 1980 for
                                          $79,900

In the appraisal process the sale price of each
comparable was adjusted for the difference that existed
between the comparable and the subject to give an
indication of the probable selling price or market
value of the subject property.

As a result of my analysis it is my opinion that your
residential property, as described above, had a market
value as of November 30, 1980, of:

          EIGHTY THOUSAND FOUR HUNDRED DOLLARS
                      ($80,400)

Should questions arise in connection with this valuation please feel free to write or call me.

I certify that I have no interest, present or contemplated, in this property.

                    Respectfully submitted

                    Fred B. Flintstone
                    Real Estate Appraiser

APPRAISAL

OF

A SINGLE FAMILY RESIDENCE

AT

4360 MANCROFT CRESCENT
REXDALE, ONTARIO

XYZ Appraisals Ltd.
436 The Kingsway
Islington, Ontario

December 15, 1980

Mr. John C. Hopeful
4360 Mancroft Crescent
Rexdale, Ontario

Dear Sir:

In response to your request I have completed an
appraisal of your residence at 4360 Mancroft Crescent,
in Rexdale, Ontario

The purpose of the appraisal was to estimate the market
value of the property, as at November 30th, 1980.

The property rights appraised are those of the "fee
simple" ownership.

As a result of my inspection, analysis and findings, it
is my considered and professional opinion that your
residential property had a market value as of November
30th, 1980, of

    EIGHTY THOUSAND FOUR HUNDRED DOLLARS
    (80,400.00)

                Respectfully submitted

                Fred B. Flintstone

Photograph of Subject Property

4360 Mancroft Crescent
Rexdale, Ontario

FRONT VIEW

SUMMARY OF SALIENT FACTS
AND IMPORTANT CONCLUSIONS

(A) ADDRESS OF PROPERTY   4360 Mancroft Crescent
Rexdale, Ontario

(B) TYPE OF PROPERTY   Single Family
Residential

(C) DATE OF APPRAISAL   November 30th, 1980

(D) SIZE OF LAND   15.24m x 37.34m
$(569.06m^2)$

(E) SIZE OF BUILDING   141.72 square metres

(F) ASSESSMENT (1980) $6,150.00

(G) 1980 MILL RATE   170.44
1980 REALTY TAXES $1,048.00

(H) ZONING   Single Family
Residential

(I) HIGHEST AND BEST USE   Single Family
Residential

(J) ESTIMATE OF LAND VALUE $55,000.00
(AS IF VACANT)

(K) ESTIMATE OF VALUE $84,000.00
BY COST APPROACH

(L) ESTIMATE OF VALUE BY $80,400.00
DIRECT SALES COMPARISON
APPROACH

(M) FINAL ESTIMATE OF VALUE $80,400.00

DEFINITION OF THE APPRAISAL PROBLEM

Purpose of Appraisal

The purpose of this appraisal is to estimate the Market Value of the subject property as of November 30th, 1980.

Market Value

The probable price at which a property will sell on the date of the appraisal, allowing a reasonable time to find a purchaser.

Effective Date of Appraisal

The effective date of this appraisal is November 30th, 1980.

Legal Description

The subject property is described as follows:

PLAN M1836
LOT 332

BOROUGH OF ETOBICOKE

Encumbrances

A mortgage of about $48,000 bearing interest at the rate of 12% per annum, repayable $503.00 monthly which includes interest and principal and maturing June 30th, 1984.

TABLE OF CONTENTS

Title Page
Letter of Transmittal
Photograph of Subject Property
Summary of Salient Facts and Important Conclusions
Definition of the Appraisal Problem

NEIGHBOURHOOD ANALYSIS

The subject property is situated in a residential
subdivision known as Martingrove Estates, a modern
housing development in the north-west sector of the
city. An analysis of the area follows.

Neighbourhood Boundaries

Martingrove Estates is a name that was associated with
this developed of houses at its initiation some 20
years ago. Since that time the name seems to have
disappeared in the association with this development.
The boundaries of the development consist of
Martingrove Road on the east, the Humber River to the
north, Highway 27 to the west and the CNR tracks to the
south.

Location of the Subject Property

The subject property as shown on the neighbourhood map
(Exhibit A) is situated more or less amidships of the
development which is uniquely devoid of any
semi-detached condominiums or rental accommodation.
This unique situation guarantees no adverse effects
from this situation. It enjoys readily available
shopping facilities and although the primary school is
somewhat removed from the area it has not proved a
hinderance in the past.

Age and History

Martingrove Estates was commenced in two phases some
twenty years ago, with subject property being in phase
II, which started eighteen years ago. The sub-divider
of phase II, who took over when the original
sub-divider was reputed to be in financial difficulty,
enjoys a good reputation. The company built its own
homes and the subject property was constructed in 1965.

Property and Occupant Analysis

The sub-division is fully built-up but recently the
Board of Education envisaging no requirement for a
primary school sub-divided and sold the site which had
been reserved for a primary school in this
neighbourhood. Homes in this area range from $75,000
to $95,000. The new homes now being constructed, being
much larger than the average, are being sold between
$120,000 and $130,000 and those backing on to the
Humber River also range as high as $120,000.

There is a good architectural range of bungalows,
split-levels and two storeys in the subject area. The
neighbourhood is considered to be in the equilibrium
stage of its life cycle, and according to the Borough
of Etobicoke Planning Staff no changes whatsoever are
contemplated.

Zoning and Land Use

The entire area is zoned single family residential with
no commercial zoning or development within its
boundaries, save for a convenience plaza of six small
stores.

The Zoning by-law in effect (R-2) is strictly enforced
and adhered to. The improved properties all appear to
be in conformity with this zoning and no adverse
effects or influences are noted.

Transportation Facilities

The Toronto Transit Commission provides a service on
Martingrove Road two blocks from the subject commencing
at 6:24 a.m. and running to 1:00 a.m. with free
transfers permitting transportation anywhere in
Metropolitan Toronto. Buses usually run every twenty
minutes, however, this is reduced during rush hours to
nine minute intervals.

Education Facilities

The neighbourhood map included in the addenda section
of this report shows the public school about 4 blocks
away and the separate school about 6 blocks. The high
school is about one mile north but the Martingrove bus
is available in inclement weather.

Shopping Facilities

There is no major shopping centre within walking
distance of the development, however, in the centre of
the development there is a small convenience plaza
consisting of a Becker's store, fish and chips store,
small fruit market, variety store, a hairdresser and a
delicatessen. Four blocks to the north is a
neighbourhood mall of approximately fifteen stores, the
major tenant being Dominion store and the rest a
variety of retail outlets including clothing, jewelry,
hairdresser, hardware, sporting, etc. The nearest
major shopping facilities would be the Albion Mall,
Rexdale Plaza and Sherway Gardens, all within easy
driving distance.

Churches

The only church within the subject boundaries is a
United Church constructed in the north east sector.
The Anglican, Catholic, and Baptist churches are
slightly over one mile away.

Parks and Playgrounds

Flagstaff Park is well located in the centre of the
development. It has access from Mercury Road and
Millview Crescent and contains a municipally operated
open air swimming pool and tennis courts along with
some minor playground equipment. A big asset is the
huge expanse of the Humber River Valley just three
blocks north for nature walks, bicycle trails, etc.

General Market Appeal

Martingrove Estates has always enjoyed good market
reaction. Homes listed for sale in 1980 enjoyed a
phenomenal success ratio in listings to sales.

Conclusion

The homes being all single family detached and well maintained makes Martingrove Estates a desirable place to live.

The stable area designation of the subject site by the Borough of Etobicoke coupled with a good mix of architectural designs makes Martingrove Estates a desirable place to live and invest. Most amenities of a desirable residential area are readily available.

The appraiser can see no adverse effects from zoning or any other change and large sales listing ratio indicates demand. Being fully developed, and the vacant areas surrounding the subject depleting rapidly, should assure demand in the forseeable future.

DESCRIPTION AND ANALYSIS OF SITE

Dimensions and Shape

The subject site is rectangular in shape with
dimensions of 15.24 metres by a depth of 37.34 metres.
It has an area of 569.06 square metres.

Topography and Drainage

This site is basically flat and approximately level
with the street. Neighbouring properties are at a
similar level and an inspection reveals no indications
of water run-off from or onto these sites. Drainage is
supplemented by the storm sewers serving the area.

Soil Characteristics

The basic soil character in the area is clay with loam
topping for landscaping purposes. There are no
indications of major settlement of the present
improvement, nor is there any indication of such a
problem in the general locale.

Services

The property is situated in an area which is considered
to be fully serviced. Underground services include
natural gas, telephone, water mains, storm sewer main
and sanitary sewer main. Television cable is also
provided on an underground basis.

There are no local improvement charges in effect; all
services being prepaid as a prerequisite of the
subdivision agreement.

Street Improvements

The street on which the property fronts is paved to a
width of 8.53m; the right-of-way being 20.12m wide and
the lot is landscaped to the road line. Improvements
include sidewalk concrete curbs and gutters.

Street lighting is by standard street lamps installed
by the developer. Sidewalks are provided on all

streets in the subdivision including the street of the subject site. Parking is permitted subject to a city by-law which limits parking to a three hour duration.

Light and Air

Being a detached home and having side yards on both sides ensures no possible obstruction to light and air.

Rights-Of-Way Easements

A search of title reveals the only right-of-way or easements affecting the subject site are those usually required in a modern subdivision for the provision of utilities such as hydro and telephone. These are not considered to adversely affect the utility of the property.

General Aspect and Appeal

The subject site may be rationally described as a standard lot, in a modern subdivision, in the Borough of Etobicoke. It is of a standard size and shape and provides good use potential. No detrimental factors are noted which would detract from its general appeal. It is not treed but there are few treed lots in the development.

Conclusion

As noted in the preceding, this is a standard lot in a typical subdivision. It is of a shape and size to provide good use potential. Full services are provided on a prepaid basis. There are no easements or right-of-ways that affect its normal utility, although such do exist, as previously noted. Good light and air characteristics are present and it may be concluded that this is an average, but desirable, residential building site.

A site plan of the property is presented as Exhibit "B" in the addenda of this report.

TAXES, ZONING AND HIGHEST AND BEST USE

Taxes

The 1980 residential mill rate (public school supporter) in the Borough of Etobicoke is 170.44 mills.

The 1980 assessment is $6,150.00 and the taxes are $1,048.21.

Zoning

According to the Borough of Etobicoke By-Law #11-737 passed on the 20th day of April 1959, the subject property is situated in an area which is zoned "Single Family Residential" (R-2). The permitted uses under this zoning designation are limited to:

    (1) One Family Dwellings
    (2) Public Parks and Schools.
    (3) Buildings and Uses Accessory to the Preceding.

The subject is in full conformity with the requirements of the existing zoning.

Highest and Best Use

It is the appraiser's opinion that the subject property as found on the date of inspection, November 30, 1980, was improved in accordance with the principle of highest and best use.

Highest and best use is defined as that use which will provide the greatest net return, in money or amenities, to the land over a given period of time.

DESCRIPTION AND ANALYSIS OF IMPROVEMENTS

The subject site, which measures 15.24m by 37.34m, is
improved with a seven room two storey house, with a
full basement, a private driveway, but no garage. It
measures 8.61 metres by 8.23 metres at ground floor
level and the two floors contain a living area of
141.72 square metres.

The building is a square plan design with the main
floor comprising the vestibule, a living room measuring
4.05m by 5.59m, a dining room 3.20m by 3.50m, a small
2-piece washroom, and a modern kitchen approximately
3.36m by 3.50m.

Interior

A staircase from the vestibule leads to the upper level
which contains a master bedroom measuring 3.66m by
4.02m, 3 other medium size bedrooms and a 4-piece
bathroom.

All interior walls and ceilings are finished drywall,
trim is painted throughout and the floors, except for
the kitchen and bathrooms, are all No. 1 oak hardwood
covered with carpeting. All rooms are painted or
decorated with a good grade of wallpaper.

The basement is open except for a tool room and a
finished recreation room. The gas fired furnace,
electric wiring and plumbing appear to be in good
repair and working order.

Exterior

The exterior is concrete block with a brick veneer
facing up to the second storey, with clapboard
sheathing at the upper level. The roof is pitched with
210 pound asphalt shingles over plywood sheathing.

Site Improvements

The entire yard is fenced and landscaped with lawns,
some shrubs and flower beds, and a small vegetable
garden at the bottom of the back yard. There is an
asphalt paved driveway, sidewalks to all entrances, and
a concrete slab patio adjacent to the rear wall of the
house.

Effective Age and General Condition

The house has been maintained in what would be
considered average to above average condition with most
repairs and maintenance being carried out periodically
and as required. As a result, it is judged to have an
effective age of 15 years and a remaining economic life
of 35 years.

A floor plan of the residence is presented as Exhibit
"C" in the addenda of this report

APPROACHES TO VALUE

In estimating the value of the subject property, two
basic approaches to value have been considered; these
are:

1. The Cost Approach
2. The Direct Sales Comparison Approach

The Cost Approach

Under this approach, first the value of the site is
estimated by comparing the subject site, as though it
were vacant, with similar sites recently sold in the
same area. Adjustments are made to the sale price of
each comparable to indicate a probable sale price or
value for the subject site. Second, the building is
costed as though it were new and actual observed
depreciation is deducted to arrive at the depreciated
cost or value of the building. Finally the value of
the site is added to the value of the building and
other improvements to obtain an estimate of the market
value of the property.

Site Valuation

In estimating the value of the site by the comparative
sales method, four reasonably similar site sales were
analyzed and adjusted to obtain an indication of the
value of the subject. The following is a detailed
description of each site.

Sale No. 1

ADDRESS: Vacant lot at 836 Amoro Drive, Etobicoke

LEGAL DESCRIPTION: Part of Lot 66R, Plan 7618
                   Etobicoke

DATE OF TRANSACTION: 6th, October 1980

DATE OF REGISTRATION: 18th, November 1980

INSTRUMENT NO.: A374836

VENDOR: Robert D. Bentley and Janet C. Bentley

PURCHASER: Ronald J. King

LOT SIZE: 15.15m x 30.48m

CONSIDERATION: $54,000 - Cash

SALE PRICE PER FRONT METRE: $3,344

REMARKS: This was a subdivided unserviced vacant lot
          Amoro Drive.

          Amoro Drive is located in an older
          neighbourhood considered to be inferior to
          the subject area. This warranted a 10%
          adjustment.

          It was similar to the subject site with
          respect to services and other physical
          features.

          The sale took place about a month before the
          valuation date and no adjustment for time was
          considered necessary.

Sale No. 2

ADDRESS: Vacant lot on Kearney Drive, Etobicoke

LEGAL DESCRIPTION: Lot 761, Plan 7621, Etobicoke

DATE OF TRANSACTION: 19th, September 1980

DATE OF REGISTRATION: 31st, October 1980

INSTRUMENT NO.: A306731

VENDOR: John C. Reed

PURCHASER: Apex Construction Co. Ltd.

LOT SIZE: 13.72m x 37.34m

CONSIDERATION: $49,600 - Cash

SALE PRICE PER FRONT METRE: $3,615

REMARKS: Similar to subject with respect to available
services and located in the same area.

No time adjustment necessary since this sale
took place about the same time as the
valuation date.

Sale No. 3

ADDRESS: Vacant lot on Mercury Road, Etobicoke

LEGAL DESCRIPTION: Lot 304, Plan M7621, Etobicoke

DATE OF TRANSACTION: 30th September, 1980

DATE OF REGISTRATION: 31st October, 1980

INSTRUMENT NO.: A324765

VENDOR: John B. Randall

PURCHASER: Build-Rite Construction Co. Limited

LOT SIZE: 13.72m x 37.34m

CONSIDERATION: $49,600 - Cash

SALE PRICE PER FRONT METRE: $3,615

REMARKS: This site is located in the immediate
neighbourhood of the subject property.

The sale took place about the same time as
the valuation date of the subject.

It was similar to the subject lot with
respect to services and all other physical
features.

Sale No. 4

ADDRESS: Vacant lot on Porterfield Road, Etobicoke

LEGAL DESCRIPTION: Lot 86, Plan M7621, Etobicoke

DATE OF TRANSACTION: November 1, 1980

DATE OF REGISTRATION: November 15, 1980

INSTRUMENT NO.: A368235

VENDOR: Frank Zapa

PURCHASER: Toro Construction Ltd.

LOT SIZE: 14.63m x 34.14m

CONSIDERATION: $52,500 - Cash

SALE PRICE PER FRONT METRE: $3,588.52

REMARKS: Similar to the subject with respect to all
physical features, and located in same
neighbourhood as subject.

This sale took place about the same time as
the effective date of this appraisal. This
site was not level, requiring a plus 1%
adjustment for grading.

Explanation of Adjustment

Time: As stated in the description of the
            comparable sites, all sales were made at
            about the same time as the effective date of
            the appraisal. Since there was no evidence
            of any market change in the value of sites
            during this short period, no time adjustment
            was considered necessary.

Location: Three comparable sales were located in the
            same general area, within a few blocks of the
            subject property. Sale No. 1 was in a poorer
            location considered to be 10% inferior to the
            subject.

Physical: All comparables except No. 4 were level
            inside lots similar to the subject requiring
            no adjustment for physical difference. As
            mentioned in the description, sale No. 4
            required some grading to level the rear
            portion of the lot thereby requiring an
            estimated 1% adjustment.

Analysis and Conclusion

The following is a tabular analysis showing the salient
information of each comparable and the necessary
adjustments and conclusion:

Sale No.	1	2	3	4
Inst. No.	A374836	A306731	A324765	A368235
Date	18-11-82	31-10-82	31-10-82	15-10-82
Sale Price	$54,000	$49,600	$49,600	$52,500
Sale Price Per Front Metre	$3,344	$3,615	$3,615	$3,589
Adjustments				
Time	-	-	-	-
Location	+ 10%	-	-	-
Physical	-	-	-	+ 1%
Total Adjustments	+ 10%			+ 1%
Adjusted Sale Price Per Front Metre	$3,678	$3,615	$3,615	$3,625

Based on the above analysis, it is concluded that the
indicated value of the subject site is $3,615 per front
metre

Value of subject site 15.24m x $3,615 = $55,093
rounded to
FIFTY FIVE THOUSAND DOLLARS
($55,000)

Reproduction Cost New

The reproduction cost new of the building was arrived
at through the use of the Boeckh Valuation Manual.
This costing manual provides a base figure per square
foot of construction for this size and type of 2-storey
building, to which is added the cost of any extras not
included in the calculation of the basic cost. The
result is multiplied by a local modified to adjust for
the date of construction and for location.

Because the cost figures are given in imperial
measurements rather than metric, the area of the
building was calculated in square footage.

Base Building Cost (Base sq. ft. Method)
2 Storey/Single Family, Detached

$$\frac{Boeckh}{Ratio} = \frac{Ground\ Floor\ Area}{Ground\ Floor\ Perimeter}$$

$$\frac{762.75\ square\ feet}{(28.25' + 27')\ x\ 2} = 6.90$$

Rounded to 7

Base Cost for Boeckh Ratio 7 = 16.03

16.03 x 1525.50 sq. ft. = $24,454

Plus 2-PC washroom   = $\underline{\quad\quad 469}$
                              $24,923

Local Reproduction Cost New

Location Modifier 1.745

$24.923 x 1.745   = $43,490

The reproduction cost new as of the effective date of
this appraisal was estimated and rounded to:

FORTY THREE THOUSAND, FIVE HUNDRED DOLLARS
($43,500)

Outside Improvements

The cost of the outside improvements including
landscaping and driveway were also estimated from
figures taken from the Boeckh Valuation Manual. Their
present day value as of the effective date of this
appraisal was $1,200.

Depreciation Analysis

The various forms of depreciation were considered, the first being physical deterioration. This has two classifications, namely curable and incurable.

Curable
A thorough inspection of the house was made for visible signs of deterioration caused by deferred maintenance. As previously stated, the house was well cared for. The only items of curable physical deterioration observed were measured for depreciation by calculating their cost to cure.

Item	Reproduction Cost New	Cost to Cure
Repairs to ceiling due to water leak	–	$650.00
Repairs to front steps	–	$250.00
		$900.00

Incurable
The measurement of depreciation under this classification of physical deterioration is broken down into two sub-headings, short lived and long lived.

The depreciation of the short lived items is calculated by finding the percentage ratio of the effective age of the component to its life expectancy and applying this percentage to the reproduction cost new of the component.

	R.C.N	Eff.Age	Life Exp.	Depreciation
Roof	$ 800	15	20	$ 600.00
Furnace	$1,600	15	20	$1,200.00
Carpeting (Bedroom)	$1,000	8	10	$ 800.00

The depreciation of the long lived components of the building are measured for depreciation by finding the percentage ratio of the effective age of the building to its total economic life and applying this percentage to the balance of the reproduction cost new of the building.

$$\frac{15}{30} (\$43,500 - \$3,400) = \$12,030$$

The next classification of depreciation considered was
functional obsolescence both curable and incurable.
This being a relatively new home built from good
architectural plans, it showed no signs of functional
obsolescence. Consequently, no depreciation was
accounted for under this classification.

Finally, depreciation was considered under the
classification of locational obsolescence. No
locational factors which would adversely affect the
value of the property were observed and no depreciation
was taken.

Summary of Cost Approach

Estimate of Site Value		$55,000
Estimate of Reproduction Cost New	$43,500	
Estimate of Accrued Depreciation		
Physical Deterioration $15,530		
Functional Obsolescence -		
Locational Obsolescence -		
Total Accrued Depreciation $15,530	$15,530	
Depreciated Cost of Building	$27,970	$27,970
Value of Outside Improvements		$ 1,200
Value of Property by Cost Approach		$84,170

round to
EIGHTY FOUR THOUSAND DOLLARS
($84,000)

DIRECT SALES COMPARISON APPROACH

This approach to value involves the process of
comparing the subject property with recent sales of
similar properties and adjusting their sales prices for
any differences. The adjusted sale of each comparable
will provide an indication of the value of the subject
property.

Presented in detail on the subsequent pages of this
report are photographs, record information and general
descriptions of four properties which have been
selected for use in this approach to value. Following
the Data Sheets is a Comparison Chart wherein the four
properties are related to the subject and adjustment to
equate dissimilarities are shown. A narration is then
presented which sets out the appraiser's rationale in
the comparison and adjustment process, leading to the
final estimate of value by this approach.

Sale No. 5

ADDRESS: 876 Kearney Drive, Rexdale

DATE OF REGISTRATION: October 30th, 1980

INSTRUMENT NUMBER: A309376

VENDOR: Robert and Joyce Rawlings

PURCHASER: Dorothy Forbes

LEGAL DESCRIPTION: Lot 842, Plan M7621, Etobicoke

LOT SIZE: 15.2m x 33.52m

AREA OF BUILDING: Approximately 145m^2

CONSIDERATION: $79,000   TERMS: $22,300 Cash

DESCRIPTION AND REMARKS: A four bedroom, 2 storey,
                          1 1/2 baths, in the same area
                          as the subject. Finished
                          recreation room, carport.
                          This home is equal in design
                          and size to the subject. Its
                          condition is inferior to the
                          subject by $1,500.
                          Furthermore, an adjustment was
                          necessary for the
                          carport and for the lack of
                          air conditioning.

Sale No. 6

ADDRESS: 697 Moonvalley Drive, Rexdale

DATE OF REGISTRATION: November 15, 1980

INSTRUMENT NUMBER: A323717

VENDOR: Patrick Doer

PURCHASER: John and Alice Smith

LEGAL DESCRIPTION: Lot 717, Plan M7635, Etobicoke

LOT SIZE   13.72m x 37.33m

AREA OF BUILDING: $143.50m^2$

CONSIDERATION: $79,900   TERMS: CASH

DESCRIPTION AND REMARKS: A four bedroom, 2-storey, 1
                           bath, no garage, in the same
                           area. Similar to subject
                           property in almost every
                           detail. No adjustments other
                           than for the lack of a second
                           bathroom were necessary.

Sale No. 7

ADDRESS: 1376 Westhumber Boulevard,
                          Rexdale

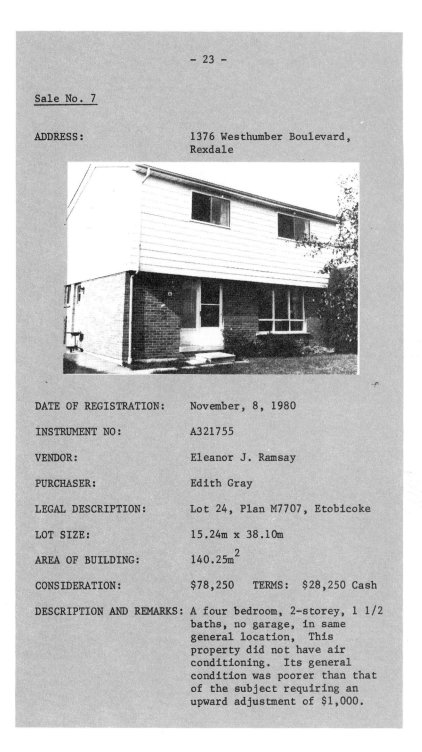

DATE OF REGISTRATION: November, 8, 1980

INSTRUMENT NO: A321755

VENDOR: Eleanor J. Ramsay

PURCHASER: Edith Gray

LEGAL DESCRIPTION: Lot 24, Plan M7707, Etobicoke

LOT SIZE: 15.24m x 38.10m

AREA OF BUILDING: $140.25m^2$

CONSIDERATION: $78,250   TERMS: $28,250 Cash

DESCRIPTION AND REMARKS: A four bedroom, 2-storey, 1 1/2
                          baths, no garage, in same
                          general location, This
                          property did not have air
                          conditioning. Its general
                          condition was poorer than that
                          of the subject requiring an
                          upward adjustment of $1,000.

Sale No. 8

ADDRESS: 3001 Pergola Road, Rexdale

DATE OF REGISTRATION: November 1st, 1980

INSTRUMENT NO: A319444

VENDOR: Brian and Mary Ashley

PURCHASER: Gordon and Rose Graham

LEGAL DESCRIPTION: Lot 92, Plan M7745, Etobicoke

LOT SIZE: 14.33m x 35.05m

AREA OF BUILDING: $141.50m^2$

CONSIDERATION: $77,900   TERMS: $25,000 Cash

DESCRIPTION AND REMARKS: A four bedroom, 2 storey, 1 bathroom, no central air conditioning, in same general area. Its condition was poorer than the subject necessitating an upward adjustment of $1,000.

Explanation of Adjustments

Time: These were all recent sales, therefore
                 no adjustment was considered necessary.

Location: All sales were in the same general
                 neighbourhood. Again, no adjustment was
                 necessary.

Lot Size: Although the comparable had slightly
                 different lot sizes, an analysis of
                 market prices did not indicate that an
                 adjustment was necessary for this
                 factor.

Carport: A study of sales in the area indicated
                 that houses with a garage or carport
                 usually sell for about $1,000 more than
                 those without a garage or carport.

Bathrooms: This type of home with a two piece
                 washroom or powder room on the main
                 floor commands a premium of $500.

Condition: Adjustment for condition is strictly a
                 matter of judgement based on the
                 estimated cost to correct any deferred
                 maintenance.

Air   A survey of comparable sales with and
Conditioning: without air conditioning indicates a
                 difference of $1,000.

Analysis of Comparable Sales

SALE NO.	5	6	7	8
SALE DATE	30-10-x0	15-11-x0	8-11-x0	1-11-x0
SALE PRICE	$79,000	$79,900	$78,250	$77,900
LOT SIZE	15.2m x 33.53m	13.72m x 37.33m	15.24m x 38.10m	14.33m x 35.05m
HOUSE AREA	145m	143.50m	140.25m	141.50m
GARAGE/CARPORT	Carport	no	no	no
REC. ROOM	yes	yes	yes	yes
BATHROOMS	1 1/2	1	1 1/2	1
CONDITION	inferior	similar	inferior	inferior
AIR CONDITIONING	no	yes	no	no

ADJUSTMENTS

TIME	nil	nil	nil	nil
TIME ADJUSTED PRICE	$79,000	$79,900	$78,250	$77,900
LOCATION	nil	nil	nil	nil
LOT SIZE	nil	nil	nil	nil
HOUSE AREA	nil	nil	nil	nil
GARAGE/CARPORT	-$1,000	nil	nil	nil
REC. ROOM	nil	nil	nil	nil
BATHROOM	nil	+$500	nil	+$500
CONDITION	+$1,500	nil	+$1,000	+$1,000
AIR CONDITIONING	+$1,000	nil	+$1,000	+$1,000
TOTAL ADJUSTMENT	+$1,500	+$500	+$2,000	+$2,500
ADJUSTED SALE PRICE	$80,500	$80,400	$80,250	$80,400

Conclusion:

The adjusted sale prices range from a low of $80,250 to a high of $80,500, a very narrow spread. The most weight was given to Sale No. 6, which indicated a probable selling price for the subject at $80,400. It was the best comparable in that it required the least number and amount of adjustment.

Therefore, value of subject property by the Direct Sales Comparison Approach was estimated at:

    EIGHTY THOUSAND FOUR HUNDRED DOLLARS
                ($80,400.)

RECONCILIATION AND FINAL ESTIMATE

Value indications:

Cost Approach $84,000.00

Direct Sales Approach $80,400.00

Cost Approach

The indication of value by the Cost Approach is clouded by the inherent difficulty of accurately estimating both the reproduction cost new and the accrued depreciation of a 15 year old home. In the market the typical purchaser does not normally think in terms of reproduction cost new less depreciation when purchasing a home of this age.

For this reason the Cost Approach has not been given full consideration although the value indication by this approach is reasonably close to and supports the value indication by the Direct Sales Comparison Approach.

Direct Sales Comparison Approach

The greatest weight has been given to the indication of value by the Direct Sales Comparison Approach because of the quality of the data on which it is based and the narrow range obtained after adjusting the comparable properties. Generally speaking the typical purchaser of a residential home like the subject would compare the sale prices of similar properties in arriving at a purchase price.

The final estimate of value as of November 30, 1980 is:

EIGHTY THOUSAND FOUR HUNDRED DOLLARS
($80,400.)
CERTIFICATION

I hereby certify that:

(a) I have personally inspected the subject property
     and considered all factors affecting the value
     thereof.

(b) The property was inspected on December 5th, 1980.

(c) I have no past, present or contemplated interest
     in the property being appraised.

(d) My opinion of the Market Value of the subject
     property as at November 30th, 1980 is:

        EIGHTY THOUSAND FOUR HUNDRED DOLLARS
            ($80,400.)

Dated: December 15, 1980   _____
                           (signature)
                           Fred B. Flintstone
                           Real Estate Appraiser

LIMITING CONDITIONS

This appraisal is made expressly subject to the conditions and assumptions as follows:

1. That the legal description as provided is correct.

2. That no responsibility is assumed for matters legal in character, nor is any opinion rendered as to title which is assumed to be marketable.

3. That the improvements are within the lot lines and that there are no encroachments from without.

4. That certain opinions, estimates, data and statistics furnished by others in the course of investigation are correct.

5. That the estimate of value herein applies only to the premises as described. Any separate valuations of land and buildings as shown must not be used for any other purposes or used separately, otherwise they are invalid.

6. That I am not required to give testimony or attendance in court by reason of the appraisal with reference to the property in question, unless arrangements have been made previously therefore.

Exhibit "A"

NEIGHBOURHOOD MAP AND SITE COMPARABLES

1. Lot 66R, Plan M 7618
   836 Amoro Drive

2. Lot 761, Plan M7621
   Kearney Drive

3. Lot 304, Plan M7621
   Mercury Road

4. Lot 86, Plan M7621
   Porterfield Road

5. Subject Site

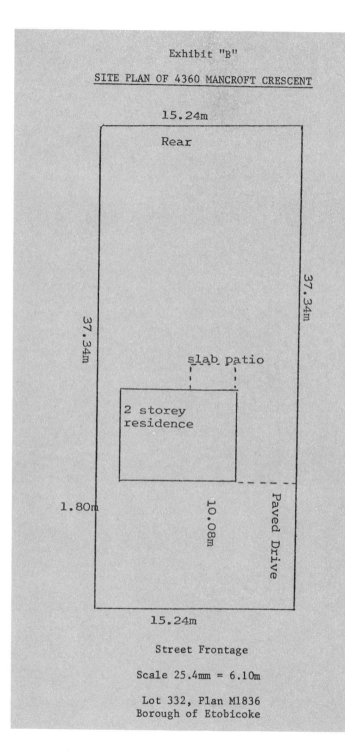

Exhibit "B"

SITE PLAN OF 4360 MANCROFT CRESCENT

15.24m

Rear

37.34m

37.34m

slab patio

2 storey
residence

1.80m

10.08m

Paved Drive

15.24m

Street Frontage

Scale 25.4mm = 6.10m

Lot 332, Plan M1836
Borough of Etobicoke

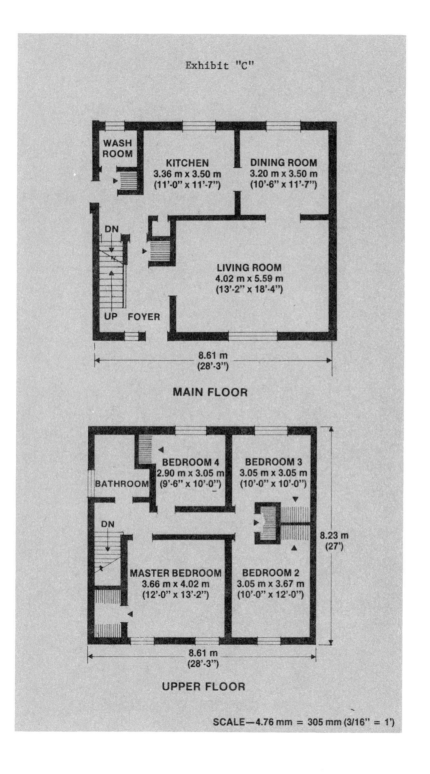

Exhibit "C"

WASH ROOM

KITCHEN
3.36 m x 3.50 m
(11'-0" x 11'-7")

DINING ROOM
3.20 m x 3.50 m
(10'-6" x 11'-7")

DN

LIVING ROOM
4.02 m x 5.59 m
(13'-2" x 18'-4")

UP   FOYER

8.61 m
(28'-3")

MAIN FLOOR

BEDROOM 4
2.90 m x 3.05 m
(9'-6" x 10'-0")

BEDROOM 3
3.05 m x 3.05 m
(10'-0" x 10'-0")

BATHROOM

DN

8.23 m
(27')

MASTER BEDROOM
3.66 m x 4.02 m
(12'-0" x 13'-2")

BEDROOM 2
3.05 m x 3.67 m
(10'-0" x 12'-0")

8.61 m
(28'-3")

UPPER FLOOR

SCALE—4.76 mm = 305 mm (3/16" = 1')

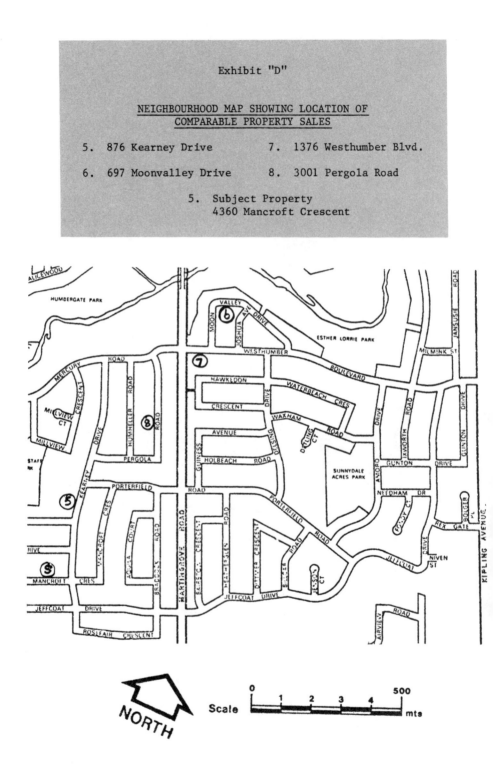

Exhibit "D"

NEIGHBOURHOOD MAP SHOWING LOCATION OF
COMPARABLE PROPERTY SALES

5. 876 Kearney Drive   7. 1376 Westhumber Blvd.

6. 697 Moonvalley Drive   8. 3001 Pergola Road

5. Subject Property
4360 Mancroft Crescent

NORTH

Scale

Index